LOVE MATCH ON THE ROAD HOME
MARGARET AMATT

LEANNAN
PRESS
INDEPENDENT PUBLISHER

LEANNAN PRESS

© **Margaret Amatt 2025**

The right of Margaret Amatt to be identified as the author of this work has been asserted in accordance with the Copyright, Designs and Patents Act 1988.

All rights reserved. No part of this publication may be reproduced, stored in a retrieval system or transmitted in any form or by any means, without the prior permission in writing of the publisher, nor to be otherwise circulated in any form of binding or cover other than that in which it is published without a similar condition, including this condition, being imposed on the subsequent purchaser.

All the characters in this book are fictitious, and any resemblance to actual persons, living or dead, is purely coincidental.

Glenbriar is a fictional town in Highland Perthshire, Scotland. Some of the historical sites and larger towns mentioned in this series are real. Homes, farms, features, and organisations are fictitious, and any resemblance to actual places or organisations is purely coincidental.

First Published by Leannan Press 2025

Book Cover designed by Margaret Amatt

eBook ISBN: 978-1-914575-27-3

Paperback ISBN: 978-1-914575-25-9

Prologue

Kerr

July

Kerr Halley skirted the island in his parents' kitchen, holding a caddy of ketchup and sauce in one hand and a packet of rolls in the other. The conservatory doors stood wide open, letting in a light breeze that carried the smell of charcoal and marinated meat. Somewhere outside, his dad barked with laughter and unleashed a string of teasing remarks at whichever unlucky neighbour had shown up early.

This house still felt the same as it always had in summer – warm, slightly chaotic, full of voices and the smell of cut grass and barbecue smoke.

Kerr set the rolls down beside a platter of burgers, and his dad clapped his shoulder. 'Good lad. Can you check if the veggie burgers are still in the kitchen? I can't find them.' He pulled a face. 'I hope I haven't mixed them in with the meat.'

Kerr raised an eyebrow. 'Oops. I'll check.' He returned to the kitchen. 'Dad reckons he might have mixed the veggie burgers with the meat ones.'

Kate Halley looked around from the fridge and closed the door. 'No, darling, he hasn't. They're right here. Oh, and can you grab the coleslaw?'

'Sure.' Kerr lifted the tray of burgers, and his mum balanced the coleslaw on top. As he headed through the living room, his attention snagged on the TV, which his dad had left playing in the background when he went to take care of the barbecue.

'...and that's Georgie Porter out of this year's Wimbledon,' the commentator was saying. *'A tough loss for the former British number one, who never quite recovered from that shoulder injury two years ago. After weeks of speculation, her early exit marks the official end of a troubled career...'*

Kerr froze halfway across the room.

The camera cut to Centre Court, and there was Georgie Porter, dark hair scraped back, sweat-drenched and sun-kissed, raising a hand to the crowd. A bittersweet smile hovered on her lips as she turned in a slow circle, waving to the stands. Her eyes looked a little watery.

Kerr's frown deepened.

He hadn't thought about her in...

Well, he *had*, obviously. Occasionally. But in the way you remember someone from another life – vaguely, cautiously, like looking at an old scar and wondering how it ever hurt that much but never poking too hard because it was a wound he definitely didn't want to reopen.

Kate came through from the kitchen and stopped. 'Kerr? What are you... Oh.'

Kerr didn't speak. He was too busy watching Georgie walk off court. Shoulders squared, chin high, just like always. Still looking completely unflappable, even in her final bow.

'Well...' Kate stepped in beside him. "That's the end of an era, isn't it?'

Kerr gave a noncommittal shrug, but his jaw tensed. 'Guess so.'

'She was good. Despite everything she did to your brother, there's no denying she was a good player when she was on form.' Kate glanced up at him. 'You ok?'

'Fine.'

But his eyes hadn't left the screen.

Georgie Porter stepped off Centre Court, gave one final wave to the crowd, then headed into the tunnel where the shade swallowed her whole. A moment later, the broadcast cut to a sideline interview. Live, the graphic in the corner said. Georgie stood in front of a branded backdrop, still in her match gear, towel slung around her shoulders, hair scraped back into a ponytail that looked a little too tight. Her smile was all white teeth and immaculate composure.

'Well, Georgie, not the ending you would've hoped for today,' the interviewer said, microphone poised. *'But an incredible career, nonetheless. How are you feeling right now?'*

Georgie gave a short laugh. *'Honestly? Like I could sleep for a week.'* She shifted her weight, one hand tugging absently at the towel. *'It hasn't really sunk in yet. I mean... I've been playing tennis professionally since I was eighteen. And now I get to figure out who I am without it.'*

'Any ideas what comes next?'

'Oh, absolutely none.' Georgie smiled again, bright but a bit lopsided this time. *'Maybe I'll do something completely mad. Buy a campervan. Drive around until I run out of road.'*

The interviewer chuckled. *'You heard it here first – keep your eyes peeled for Georgie Porter cruising up to a beach near you.'*

Kate made a polite noise in her throat, something between a laugh and a scoff. 'Well, I don't see that happening. But then she always was unpredictable.'

Kerr was too busy watching Georgie's face to say anything. Her posture was perfect, media-trained and polished. But there was something off in her eyes. So what? She was nothing to him. Never had been.

The way she'd dumped his brother, Jake, was cruel. The crush Kerr had nursed for her long before she dated Jake still stung, and all the years he'd spent trying not to wonder *what if* were a waste... But even now, a part of him cared.

He didn't want to. God, he *really* didn't want to. But his brain had already queued the memories like a greatest hits reel. No matter who he'd dated since, he'd always had a weird sense of something unresolved. Something, if he investigated closely enough, he could trace back to Georgie. A very one-sided something.

Kate's voice cut into Kerr's thoughts. 'She made her choices. Thankfully, Jake moved on – eventually.'

Kerr gave a slow nod. 'Yeah.' Though he wasn't a hundred per cent convinced. The Jake and Georgie saga had an unfinished air about it.

The interview ended. Georgie turned from the camera, waving again to the crowd of press behind the barrier, before disappearing into the depths of the All England Club for the last time. The screen cut to a panel of commentators dissecting her legacy, stats flashing across the bottom.

Kerr finally looked away and headed into the garden with the burgers and the coleslaw.

'Campervan,' he muttered under his breath as he passed through the doors into the sunlight. 'Whatever.'

What she did was her business, and it was unlikely to affect him or his family ever again.

And just as well.

Chapter One

Georgie

September

Georgie Porter rested her hand on the warm, sun-baked side of the campervan, fingers splayed against the curved metal painted in cheery cream and orange. It looked like something from a whimsical travel blog, all floral decals and retro charm. Once, she'd posed in designer tennis whites next to vintage sports cars and yachts, smiling for the cameras on windswept clifftops or sun-drenched courts. Now she stood in a sage green jumpsuit next to the van parked not in Monaco or Melbourne, but on the dull grey tarmac of her parents' suburban London driveway.

She massaged a rising niggle in her chest. There would be no more photoshoots like that. She'd never again feel the thrill of beating a top-ten player or play on Centre Court at Wimbledon.

'Are you absolutely certain about this?' Her mother appeared at the front door, forehead creased with concern. 'Living in a van seems so… unstable.'

'It's not living in a van, Mum. It's travelling. There's a difference.' Georgie smiled to soften her words, knowing her mother's worry came from love, even if it sometimes felt like suffocation. 'I want to do something different.'

Her father joined them, shielding his eyes from the sun. 'Are you sure the battery's been checked?'

'Yes, Dad.'

'And the tyres?'

'The garage gave her a full check.'

'Her?' Her mum pulled a face. 'You're not going to go all quirky on us and give it a name and assign it a gender, are you?'

'That's not quirky. That's normal. Everyone with a van does it.' Or they did in books anyway. She'd read a lot of them. On tour, there had been plenty of time for it. She loved novels where the heroine got a campervan and set off on a journey of discovery. This was her version of it... or possibly just her post-retirement crisis playing out. When your career ended at thirty, it wasn't exactly an easy adjustment to make.

She was allowed some kind of breakdown. As long as it wasn't in the van.

'What have you named her then?' her father asked.

Georgie laughed. 'I haven't decided yet... Maybe I'll go with Ayu.'

'With what?'

'Ayu. As Yet Unnamed.'

Her father shook his head. 'I don't see why you couldn't just rent a holiday cottage like normal people.'

Normal people. She couldn't remember what being a 'normal' person was. Since she was eighteen, she'd had people managing her every move. Her only freedom had been on the court. Now that she had so much of it, it was like being swept away in a flood.

'It'll be fun,' she said. 'And I can afford it, so why not?'

Her mother stepped closer, adjusting the collar of Georgie's denim jacket even though it didn't need adjusting. 'And you're sure you don't want to wait until after Ethan and Cara bring the baby over next weekend? They'd love to see you before you go.'

'I already said goodbye to them.' Georgie's brother and his wife had brought a new distraction into her parents' lives, leaving Georgie feeling oddly displaced. Neither of her parents were particularly demonstrative – or they never had been with her. Her successes were what brought them the most joy, but now that happiness came in the form of a two-month-old bundle. And the timing couldn't be better. With her parents content with their next project, Georgie was ready for her solo adventure. 'And I'm not going forever. Just... a few weeks.'

Her father frowned. Doing anything without a plan wasn't his style. But Georgie *had* a plan. Just not one she was ready to share. Not with him. Not with anyone.

Because it involved risk – and she wasn't sure anyone else would understand.

She may have joked in her retiral interview about the campervan dream, but there was method in the madness – or kind of.

'I'd better get going.' Georgie reached for the van door.

Her mother stepped in and pulled her into a hug that smelled of Chanel No. 5. 'Please be careful, darling. And call us when you stop.'

'I will.'

Her father's hug was briefer and more restrained, but no less genuine. 'Drive safely. And if that engine makes any funny noises—'

'I'll get it checked straight away.'

They stepped back, and for a moment, Georgie saw them through the eyes of a stranger: a well-dressed couple in their sixties, standing on the pavement outside a smart suburban London home, waving off their daughter in a campervan. A perfectly normal family scene – except this was probably the strangest thing she'd ever done.

She'd only learned to drive two years ago. She'd never camped in her life. And she'd never gone anywhere alone – without her parents, a coach, a physio, an agent, or a manager tracking her every move.

She climbed into the driver's seat, adjusted her sunglasses on the top of her head, and started the engine. It came to life with a reassuring purr.

'Love you!' she called through the open window.

'Love you too,' they chorused, and she waved before pulling away from the kerb, watching them shrink in her rear-view mirror until they disappeared.

The streets of Northwood slid past, the van stop-starting at every traffic light as she made her way to the quieter back road that led north. If she could avoid motorways, she would. The van had been thoroughly checked, but Georgie wasn't confident pushing her above fifty-five miles an hour. That seemed the speed she was built for – and Georgie was ok with that.

Admitting she still found driving a little scary didn't seem wise when she'd just embarked on a solo road trip. But she'd always lived by the motto: *feel the fear and do it anyway*. Almost always anyway. And that was exactly what she planned to do.

The traffic thinned as she left the city behind, her hands relaxing on the steering wheel as the road unfurled like a ribbon ahead of her, winding through a patchwork of fields. With no schedule to keep and no one to answer to, Georgie took her time, meandering through villages with flower-decked pubs and watching cows drowse on sun-warmed slopes.

She flicked through playlists, settling on a mix of easy-going pop and guilty-pleasure throwbacks. It wasn't long before she was singing at the top of her lungs, drumming her fingers against the wheel in time with the beat. Her voice was rusty – she hadn't belted out a tune like this in ages – but it felt good. Freeing.

Later, she stopped for lunch somewhere in the Midlands, and she switched to an audiobook she'd downloaded. The spice was exquisite, and she had to remember to watch the road as things heated up between the couple. This was a different type of story to the softer ones about girls with their campervans, but she unashamedly loved both, depending on her mood.

A hot scene was in full flow when she rolled into a quiet town and noticed an old man walking his dog glance sharply in her direction. Georgie squeaked, scrambling to turn the volume down. The window was wide open.

Oops.

Oh, well, so what? It wasn't like she needed to keep up her public image now.

The landscape began to change as she got further into the north of England, hills rising steeper and stone walls lining the road. The distant silhouette of fells marked the edge of the Lake District.

This was where she'd decided to make her first stop. She gripped the wheel a little tighter and took a steadying breath. Tonight would be the real test – her first night alone in the van. No hotels, no staff, no fans. Just her, a pull-out bed, and a bowl of pasta if she could figure out how to light the stove.

The sudden quiet filled the van, and it felt like her mind had been waiting for it – because almost at once, it leapt to him.

Jake.

The real reason she was doing this trip.

She hadn't let herself think about him properly in years, had trained herself not to. But now, with every mile bringing her closer to Scotland, closer to Glenbriar, it was impossible to push him aside.

Jake Halley. Her first boyfriend. And hell, did she owe him an apology? A huge one. Out of everything that had malfunctioned in her tennis career, nothing left such a bitter taste as what had happened with Jake. Painful things, shameful things – things she wished she could erase. Things she knew Jake wouldn't have forgotten. Or forgiven.

She had to see him. Had to explain. It was the only way she could fully close this chapter and move forward.

Where to, she had no idea. But at least her heart would finally be free to figure it out.

Chapter Two

Kerr

Kerr burst into the Glenbriar High School staffroom, kicked the door shut with the heel of his boot, and made a beeline for the kettle like a man on a mission. Heads turned, including Deputy Head Adele, perched elegantly at the corner table with her tablet and herbal tea. Her sleek black hair was twisted into an elegant updo. Immaculately dressed in tailored navy and soft cream, with nails that gleamed like they'd been professionally polished that morning, she raised one perfectly arched brow at him. Even without speaking, Adele's expression had the power to stop students – and adults – in their tracks. Kerr raised his hands in surrender.

'Sorry. Just had a shit morning.' Three third years had decided to treat his classroom like a wrestling ring, and as for Max Lyndell... Kerr's jaw was so set he almost cracked a tooth thinking about that student. He was *that* pupil. The one every teacher dreaded having in their class. And Kerr was one of the unlucky ones this year.

'Please tell me it wasn't Max.' Adele barely restrained an eye roll.

'No can do.' Kerr poured a mug of coffee. 'It *was* Max.'

Adele groaned. 'Do I need to contact his parents again? I really hope not, because they drive me insane.'

'Na.' Kerr slumped into the seat next to history teacher Eddie. 'It was just low-level stuff, but it's so disruptive.'

'I'm sorry to hear it.' Eddie sipped his green tea. 'Though I feel very blessed that Max decided not to take history.'

'Bastard,' Kerr muttered, catching his eye, and they both laughed. Kerr swallowed a mouthful of coffee, then leaned his head on Eddie, pretending to sleep. 'Was I an annoying twat like that when I was here?'

'A hundred times worse,' Eddie said.

Kerr snorted and jolted up, laughing. Eddie had taught at Glenbriar High School forever, and he still looked dapper and fit in his late fifties. He'd been Kerr's teacher years ago, and now Kerr was privileged enough to call him a friend.

'I've got some more bad news for you unfortunately,' Eddie said.

'Oh, what?' Kerr eyed him, running a hand through his hair; it was getting long – longer than he usually wore it anyway.

'Tennis Club drama.'

Kerr closed his eyes. 'Please tell me they've cancelled the tournament and turned the courts into a beer garden.'

'Not quite. Antonia's quit the committee.'

Kerr blinked. 'Seriously?' Antonia was down as his mixed doubles partner for the next match day, though she babied him so much it was worse than partnering his mum. 'But she's still playing at the match day, right?'

'Wrong.' Eddie gave a regretful shrug.

Kerr groaned and let his head fall back. 'Well, that's it then. I'm done. Retired. I'll donate my racquet to charity and become a couch pundit.'

'You can't bail.' Eddie nudged Kerr's foot with his own. 'I still need you for the men's doubles.'

'Ugh.' Kerr rubbed his forehead. 'Can I get my mum to write a note saying I'm ill?'

'No, you bloody can't.'

'Oh, fuck.'

'Language, Mr Halley.' Adele waved a manicured nail at him. 'You'll scare off the new staff.'

She nodded towards the kettle, where a new member of staff, with long golden hair, and the hilariously cute name of Mirren Elphinstone, was attempting to locate a clean mug among the archaeological layers of the staffroom sink.

'She's used to me already,' Kerr said. Mirren was a music teacher, but they'd already bonded over shared breakdowns about Max, who they both had the misfortune of teaching.

Clara Morgan, the guidance teacher, pointed her to the shelf of spares. 'Take one from this shelf.' She caught Kerr's eyes and smiled. He returned it. Clara was a sweetie and always helped everyone.

'Do you play tennis?' Kerr asked her, glancing over his shoulder.

'Um...' Clara frowned and tucked her neat brown hair behind her ear. 'Not really.'

'Do any of you lovely ladies play tennis?' Kerr asked. 'And more specifically, would any of you want to partner me in the mixed doubles event?'

'Looks like you're out of luck.' Eddie glanced around. People were apologetically shaking their heads.

'Bums,' Kerr muttered. 'Might be best if I pull out of that event.'

Clara sat down opposite him, a rather pained expression growing on her usually smiley face. 'I wish I'd learned to play now.'

Eddie pulled out a chair for Mirren. 'How are you getting on so far?'

'Good, thanks.' Mirren adjusted her honey-blonde hair, pulling it into a ponytail. 'I have mostly good students.'

'Except Max,' Kerr said.

'Yeah, pretty much.'

'You don't play tennis, do you?'

'No, I'm more into music. My boyfriend's in a band. They're playing at the pub this week. They're called Tavrach. You might have heard of them. They're pretty good, if anyone fancies coming along.'

'Yeah, I know them, well, not personally, but I often go to watch them.' Kerr twisted the ring on his index finger. 'They're great.'

'They're desperately looking for someone to handle the sound tech for the Autumn Gold Festival,' Mirren said. 'I said I would help, but I'm not that great at the tech, and my boyfriend doesn't really want me involved. Tavrach is *his* thing. He'd rather I just came along and watched.'

Kerr thought that a bit odd, but couldn't question it as Eddie nudged him, saying, 'You could do it.'

Kerr hesitated. But why not? He loved their music, and the festival was a highlight of Glenbriar's calendar. He'd been meaning to get more involved ever since he came back.

'Yeah, I could help out,' he offered.

Mirren beamed. 'I'll let my boyfriend know. Can I give him your number?'

'Sure.'

The bell rang, sending them all scattering to their respective classrooms. Kerr gave Mirren his number and got up. Clara was watching him across the room with a distant look. He smiled at her before returning to class.

It was a manic day and, by the time he got home to his little house on Kirk Lane, he was knackered. He kicked off his trainers and hung his jacket on a hook in the narrow hallway. It opened to a living room that managed to be both cosy and sparse: a charcoal grey sofa facing a wall-mounted TV, a coffee table cleared of everything except a few books and a gaming controller, bookshelves filled with an eclectic mix of sci-fi paperbacks and textbooks.

Kerr shrugged off his shirt, leaving just his white tee, and headed to the kitchen. Like the rest of the house, it was functional rather than fancy. Everything here was compact. It had to be. The houses on Kirk Lane were cute and quirky looking but inside they were small and a little awkward. But with properties hard to come by in Glenbriar, Kerr was lucky to have snapped this place up in the summer.

The woman who had owned it before was engaged to the minister and now lived in the Manse just up the road. There had to be a good story there.

Dinner was a microwaveable Thai curry that actually tasted pretty good. Kerr wasn't a terrible cook, but cooking elaborate meals for one person always felt like too much effort for too little reward. He'd save his culinary ambitions for when he had someone to impress. And hopefully that would happen, though he'd put dating on hold for a bit while he healed from a pretty shit breakup that had knocked him sideways. He hadn't quite found his way since.

He was halfway through his dinner when the doorbell rang. Who the hell? Nobody ever really called round unannounced. Even his mum messaged first, and he wasn't expecting a delivery.

He toyed with the idea of ignoring it, but then he'd wonder who it was.

Leaving his half-eaten meal on the tiny kitchen table, he headed to the door. He could only make out a silhouette through the frosted glass panel. Medium height, slight build.

He turned the lock and pulled the door open.

Time did that weird thing where it stretched and compressed simultaneously. One heartbeat seemed to last ages, and yet he couldn't quite process what he was seeing.

Georgie Porter stood on his doorstep.

He recognised her immediately – how could he not? But his brain struggled to make sense of why she was here.

'Hi.' Her brow furrowed. 'It's Kerr, isn't it?'

'It was the last time I checked.'

She gave a little smile, then sucked on her lower lip. 'And Jake... Is he here?'

'Jake's in London.' Kerr folded his arms. 'What's this all about?'

'I just—' She shifted her weight, adjusting the strap of the bag slung across her body. 'It's complicated.'

Complicated? That word seemed too delicate for what was happening. Kerr's heart tremored. Something weird was going on, and he couldn't imagine it would lead to anything good. Did it ever where Georgie was concerned?

Chapter Three

Georgie

Georgie shifted her weight, suddenly aware of how ridiculous this must seem.

'I, um, I thought this was Jake's place.'

'I'm not sure why you'd think that. Or even how you got this address.' Kerr unfolded his arms and leaned his hand on the doorframe.

Eek. This was getting worse. How she'd got this address wasn't exactly legit – it had involved some almost stalkerish behaviour after hearing her mum talking with an old friend. The friend had said Kate's son had moved back to Glenbriar and was now living on Kirk Lane. Georgie had frantically googled all recent property sales and new lets, and this one had come up.

But of course, Kate had two sons.

And the fact that Kerr Halley was the one standing here complicated things.

'Oh. A friend told me... well, told my mum. She must have muddled you up with Jake.' They did look alike, after all – both tall, very handsome, broad-shouldered with dark hair and brooding looks. Jake did anyway. He did brooding like a champ. And from the look on Kerr's face, he wasn't far off. His brow was furrowed, and his eyes narrowed.

'I wonder if you could give him a message for me?'

How annoying was it that Jake was in London? How long had he been that close, and she hadn't realised?

'Depends on what it is.' Kerr stayed firmly positioned in the doorway.

'Could you tell him I'd really like to talk to him? Obviously not here. But when I get back to London.'

Something in Kerr's expression shifted. He studied her face for a moment.

'I'll let him know. But I can't promise anything. He's engaged now, you know.'

The news hit her like a physical blow, though she kept her expression neutral.

'That's... wow. Great.'

And it was good to know he'd moved on, but it threw up yet more complications. Would closure for her do nothing more than reopen old wounds for him? Maybe she should just let sleeping dogs lie.

Kerr nodded. 'I'll pass on your message. Are you staying in town?'

'At Heather Glen,' she replied. 'I've got a campervan. I'm sort of... on a road trip.'

He raised his eyebrows and opened his mouth, then closed it again before any words came out.

An awkward pause ensued, filled only by the distant sound of birds and the soft rustle of leaves from the garden.

'Well...' Georgie took a step back. 'Thank you. For, um, that.'

'No problem.' Kerr leaned against the doorframe, one hand braced above his head. The angle made his shirt stretch slightly across his chest, and a tousled strand of dark hair fell across his brow. 'Shouldn't you give me your number? Otherwise, I won't be able to tell you what Jake says.'

'Of course, yes.'

He pulled a phone from his pocket, and she said her number. He keyed it in.

He was younger than her. When they'd been in high school, she'd often seen him. He'd smiled at her sometimes, even occasionally made jokes, which was something his brother rarely did, but she hadn't spoken much to him. When she'd dated Jake, Kerr hadn't been around much. Georgie had left Glenbriar to go to tennis academy just months after she and Jake started going out together. She'd never expected her relationship with Jake to last, but he was convinced they could do long distance. She'd tried because being able to say she had a boyfriend was a great way to ward off questions. But with a career so carefully curated, she had very little time to see Jake. All they did was talk on the phone and message.

'Right, then...' Kerr gave a little shrug. 'I'll let you know what he says, but just so you know, I doubt he'll be that receptive to whatever it is you have to say.'

She nodded. 'Yeah. I get that. But ask him, please?'

Her eyes met his, and inside her mind, memories started rolling like an old movie. Georgie pulled in a breath. There was that one time she'd come back to Scotland for Jake's graduation party. It was the first time they'd seen each other in forever, but Jake had had too much to drink, and Georgie wanted to get away. She'd run into Kerr. For a long, charged moment, they'd looked at each other, just as they were looking at each other now.

Georgie couldn't do anything with Jake after that. It seemed wrong, though she wasn't sure why. She should have broken it off with him there and then, but she always felt sorry for him – and a little afraid of what he might do to himself – and couldn't bring herself to do it. They'd stayed together for a while longer... only for their relationship to end in the most horrible way.

'I'll let you know what he says,' Kerr broke the connection. 'See you.'

'Yeah, thanks.' She gave a little wave as the door closed.

As she walked back to her van, she sighed. Ok, none of that was what she'd hoped for, but she wasn't at the end of the tunnel yet.

The road to Heather Glen twisted alongside Loch Briar, each bend unveiling a fresh sweep of beauty – glass-still water mirroring the fiery blaze of hillside trees, their leaves gold, amber and deep crimson. Wisps of mist clung to the loch's edge, softening the jagged outlines of the hills beyond. Clusters of bracken rustled in the breeze, their coppery fronds bending low along the verge. Georgie drank in as much of the familiar landscape as she could, but the memory of Kerr's voice and the look in his eyes looped through her thoughts, louder and more vivid than anything outside the window.

A wooden sign marked the entrance to Heather Glen Campsite & Water Sports Centre. Georgie followed the gravel drive past a cluster of tents and caravans until she reached a small reception building. Laughter drifted from somewhere nearby, along with the shouts of kids playing. It should have felt welcoming. Instead, it made her chest ache with the knowledge that wherever she went, she didn't really belong.

Maybe she'd half hoped that, in coming back here, she'd step into an old life – the last place she really remembered actually feeling like home, and not just a hotel room somewhere in the world.

She parked her campervan and stepped out. The door swung open before she reached it, and a man bounded out, all energy and broad smiles.

'Oh, hey. I was just about to do my evening rounds, but let me check you in first. I'm Logan. Welcome to Heather Glen.'

He looked about her age, maybe a bit older, with sun-weathered skin and the lean build of someone who spent time outdoors and being active. His enthusiasm was so genuine that Georgie found herself smiling back despite herself.

'Thank you. I messaged about a pitch for my campervan.'

'Yes, I remember.' Logan gestured for her to follow him back inside. 'Let me just get you a map and I'll go over the site rules.'

The reception was small but warm, with maps of walking trails pinned to cork boards and photos of people kayaking and paddleboarding on the loch.

'So...' Logan pulled out a site map and drew a cross on it. 'I've put you here. It's near the woods – a bit more private than some of our other pitches – and you'll have the stream on one side. Good spot for someone who wants a bit of peace but doesn't mind a five-minute walk to the showers.' He glanced up. 'That sound all right?'

'Sounds perfect,' Georgie said. 'The van has a shower, but it's pretty tiny.'

All of this was still new. A total novelty compared to everything she'd been used to. No doubt it would wear off, but the sense of freedom was incredible.

Logan handed her a small welcome pack and led her back outside, pointing the way to her pitch.

'Any problems, just give a shout. My wife, Eleanor, or I are usually around.'

Georgie thanked him and climbed back into her van, following his directions through the site. The pitch was a level patch of grass backed by silver birch and rowan trees, with a burbling stream marking the boundary. It felt sheltered – hidden from the main site but still connected to it.

Georgie backed the van into position, taking care to leave enough room for her fold-out awning. She connected the hookups and pulled out her portable table and chair.

Her former agent thought she should do a travel blog and document her travels to keep herself in the public eye in case she wanted to go into commentary next, which seemed like the logical progression. But Georgie refused. This trip was exactly the opposite of being in the public eye. She wanted to hide. Be normal. Be herself.

She filled the kettle and set it to boil, then pulled ingredients from the fridge for a simple pasta dish. As she chopped tomatoes and basil, her mind drifted back to Kerr and Jake.

Nine years ago, not long after the graduation party, she'd made a choice that still haunted her. Her coach and manager had convinced her that a public relationship with rising men's tennis star Stefan Varis would revive both their careers after a dip in form. At the time, it had seemed like a smart move – she'd been desperate to stay relevant.

So things with Jake had to end. In truth, she'd been relieved it was over. If she'd had the guts to end it earlier – or never said yes to him at all – everything would have been easier.

But worst of all, she hadn't even ended it herself. Her manager had promised to do it for her, but he hadn't – Jake had found out on TV along with the rest of the world.

The one time she'd truly felt the fear and failed to act. It sat heavily on her even now. The need to apologise still burned deep.

Draining the pasta, she tossed it with the tomatoes and olive oil, then took her plate and a glass of wine outside and sat facing the stream.

Stefan had turned out to be nice. They were still friends. When they'd been involved in the fake-dating scam, they'd found it easy to play along because they understood each other. There was no great passion, but they'd rubbed along – even lost their virginity together rather unspectacularly in Monte Carlo.

She stabbed her pasta. All that seemed like something bizarre from another life now. A life where nothing had made sense, and yet it made a lot more sense than what she was doing now.

A pang of complete emptiness rose inside her, and she swallowed it away.

What was she going to do with her life?

She was living the moment she'd never really thought would come – never prepared for.

Was there life after tennis?

If so, where? Doing what? With whom? And when?

While there was great freedom in doing this, it couldn't wash away the massive block of uncertainty standing in her path.

Chapter Four

Kerr

'Morning.' Eddie's voice carried across the staffroom as Kerr traipsed over to him. 'You look like you could use this more than me.' He handed him a fresh mug of coffee.

'Legend.' Kerr accepted the coffee with a grateful nod and slid into a chair next to Clara, who greeted him with a quiet smile.

Across the table, the new English teacher, Sam Addison, was mid-flow, his deep voice rumbling through some story or other. Adele sat still, fingers curled around her mug but not drinking, her eyes fixed on his face like she was following every syllable. When he paused to smile, she blinked as if surfacing from a trance and gave a slightly breathless laugh.

Clara too had seemed entranced by Sam's voice before Kerr sat down, but she flipped her attention to him and studied him over the rim of her mug.

'Are you ok?' she asked. 'Did you have Max again?'

'No, I'm just tired,' Kerr replied. And it wasn't a lie. He'd lain awake half the night thinking about Georgie Porter. Memories he'd thought he'd buried had crawled out of their graves and were hammering on the inside of his head. She was back.

Back, and wanting to talk to Jake. Of course, they had unresolved issues. Kerr would just sit on the sidelines and watch – as he always did. Like a spectator at one of her matches.

Eddie sat on the other side of Kerr with his own mug of coffee. 'Spill.' He raised an eyebrow at Kerr. 'I've known you since you were thirteen, and I know your "something's bothering me but I'm pretending it's not" face.' He leaned back in his chair. 'Out with it.'

Kerr stared into his coffee. Part of him wanted to brush it off, to keep Georgie's appearance – and all the complicated feelings it stirred – to himself. But another part was desperate to unload the weight that had settled on his shoulders.

'Do you remember Georgie Porter?'

'How could I forget?' Eddie took a sip of coffee. 'One of our most famous former pupils.'

'I don't know how much attention you paid to who was dating whom back then. Or if you know that Georgie dated my brother.'

'Ah, right.' Eddie gave a little nod. 'I think I remember something about it. Why?'

'Because she turned up at my door last night, looking for him.'

Clara gasped. 'What? Isn't she a tennis player?'

'Yeah.' Kerr ran a hand through his hair. 'She's just retired.'

Eddie frowned, leaning forward. 'What did she want to speak to him about? I mean, it was a long time ago, though it amazes me how fast ten or so years can whizz by.'

'They dated after she left. Tried long distance. Jake applied for a job based in London that he could also do remotely, so he could travel with her on tour. Then she fucked off with another tennis player and broke his heart. He's engaged now, and it's taken him a long time to get over it. I'm not sure he'll want to speak to her. I don't even know if I should tell him.'

Kerr delivered the story from a supportive brother's point of view – and he was. He fully understood how gutted Jake felt when Georgie went off with someone else. Just as gutted as Kerr had been when Jake had asked out the girl Kerr had fancied since almost his first day at high school. He'd like to say it was a coincidence, but Jake knew. He pretended he didn't, but Kerr had told him. After they started dating, Jake claimed not to remember.

Convenient.

Still, Kerr had only been a young teenager. What did it matter? A lot had gone on in between. Including that time at Jake's graduation when he and Georgie had shared a look so intense they'd almost started a fire... and last evening, it had happened again. But so what? It wasn't like she was interested in him. She'd made her choice long ago – probably didn't even remember he existed.

'Yes, that's a dilemma.' Eddie pulled a face. 'But once she realised Jake wasn't there, didn't she just go away again?'

'She did, but she wants me to speak to him and tell him she wants to talk.'

'Do you think your brother will be upset about that?' Clara asked. 'Can't he just say no if he doesn't want to speak to her?'

'He can, but... well, he's touchy about anyone even mentioning her.' Which hadn't been easy. His whole family enjoyed playing and watching tennis. Georgie's memory often hung around like the elephant in the room.

'It's a shame you're caught in the middle,' Clara said.

Eddie patted Kerr's shoulder. 'I think you should just deliver the message, then step back.'

Which he would; only he knew his brother. Even speaking about something like this would be like ramming a metal rod into an open wound.

'I'll message him at lunchtime.' He drained his coffee. Right now, he had twenty-eight S3s to deal with – including Max Lyndell.

As he left the staffroom, a tall, rather gangly sixth-year boy approached him. 'Mr Halley.' He half looked at his feet as he spoke.

'Hi, Grieg. What's up?'

'I have to go to the dentist in the afternoon, so I'll miss class, but I don't want to miss anything important for my project.'

'You can catch up at home. I'll email you the notes.'

Greig looked up and nodded. 'Thanks.'

'No worries.' Kerr headed on to his classroom. It hummed with the particular energy of twenty-eight teenagers who'd just come from break – a mixture of sugar crashes, hormonal spikes, and voices that hadn't been modified to suit the classroom.

'Right, come on.' Kerr moved between the desks where pupils were opening laptops, hyperaware of the quiet snickers from the back corner where Max Lyndell held court. 'Break's over, time to focus.'

Sunlight streamed through the high windows, making the room feel like a mini oven. Kerr threw one open.

'I need you all to open the game design you were working on last class, then I'll talk you through a short clip on the next part of the integration.'

From the back, a loud sigh cut through the moment.

'Problem, Max?' Kerr asked.

Max lounged in his chair, the sleeves of his school shirt rolled up to reveal tanned wrists. His tie hung loose and askew, like an afterthought. Kerr had to remind himself this boy was the age Kerr was when he'd pined after Georgie. A hormonal teenager who knew nothing. So holding onto some crazy memory was silly. 'Just wondering when we're gonna learn something useful, sir.'

'Depends on what you consider useful,' Kerr said. 'If you don't enjoy gaming, that's fine. I assume you don't have a PlayStation or anything like that?'

Several students snickered.

'He does,' another boy said. 'And a Switch, and an Xbox.'

'There you go then,' Kerr said. 'And all the games you play on them were designed by people who understand what we're learning about just now. It's a very lucrative industry. But if it doesn't interest you, you can always discuss a change of subjects. As you've just started S3, there might be a chance to switch.'

'Na, it's ok.' Max shrugged.

'Good.' Kerr talked through a short intro film and walked them through the coding process they were working on. Soon the classroom settled into a productive buzz. Students clustered around their desks, heads bent together in consultation. He moved between groups, offering guidance, asking questions that pushed their thinking without giving away answers.

'Jack, turn around, please.' Kerr watched the boy as he looked over his shoulder to giggle at Max. 'If you're having difficulty, I'll help you, or you can ask someone in your own group.' Kerr had deliberately separated this duo.

As the lesson progressed, Max's disruptions grew more frequent, as they always did – a cough just loud enough to interrupt, a whispered comment that set his tablemates snickering, the constant click-click-click of the mouse being pressed rapidly.

When Kerr returned to the front to discuss the next steps, Max leaned back in his chair until it balanced on two legs, his posture a study in calculated boredom. 'Teachers always think they know everything,' he muttered.

The class went quiet, heads turning to gauge Kerr's reaction. He felt twenty-seven pairs of eyes on him, waiting.

'Interesting theory, Max.' Kerr set down his marker. 'Speaking as someone who has spent six years teaching, I can confidently say I know almost nothing about "everything."' He moved to Max's table, pushing back the screen on his laptop. 'What I do know is that if you concentrated a lot more, you'd have got a lot further than this. Next lesson, if you can't work without disrupting your group, you can work on your own. And if that doesn't work, then we'll have to seriously consider you transferring to a different class. There's no point in choosing a subject, then showing up and refusing to work.'

Max's cheeks flushed, but there was a flicker of something else in his eyes – resentment or anger perhaps.

'I am working,' he muttered.

'Just make sure what you're working on has something to do with what we're learning.'

Kerr circulated again, offering guidance and encouragement, but keeping an eye on Max.

'Five minutes to pack up,' he called eventually. 'Make sure you have saved everything before shutting down the computers.'

The lunch bell rang, releasing a flood of teenagers into the corridor. Kerr remained at his desk, listening to the tide of voices ebb away. After taking a moment to breathe, he pulled his phone from his pocket and set it on the desk. Then he pulled up Jake's contact. Jake didn't always appreciate random calls – though he was guilty of doing it himself when *he* thought it a good time. Still, Kerr didn't fancy rocking the boat, so a message would do. And actually it would be a lot easier to fire off a message and not have to be there when the fallout happened...

He typed out a few words, then deleted them. Started again. Deleted again.

He ran a hand through his hair, frustrated with himself. This wasn't complicated. It was a simple message. Information to pass along, nothing more.

He couldn't stop seeing Georgie's face. And damn it, he couldn't stop thinking about her. That had always been a problem. Jake's asking her out in the first place had been a niggling source of irritation all through his high school life.

Thankfully it had stopped when he'd started dating Anna.

'For God's sake,' he muttered to himself. He didn't need to remind himself that his whole dating history was a dumpster fire. 'Just send the message.'

His thumbs hovered over the screen for a moment longer before he finally typed the message.

KERR: Hey! Got a bit of a shock yesterday. Georgie Porter turned up at my door. She was looking for you. I didn't give her your contact – just said I'd pass on a message that she would like to talk to you. I told her that wasn't likely but am doing what I said I would.

Kerr pressed send before he could overthink it further. The message whooshed away, and he set his phone down. Done.

Hopefully Jake would say no, and that would be the end of the whole business.

But the knot in his stomach didn't ease.

No matter what Jake said, it didn't remove the knowledge that Georgie was here. In Glenbriar. So close.

Why did that even matter?

He let out a sigh and got to his feet. Maybe he just needed food, and then he'd be fine.

His phone buzzed as he headed down the corridor towards the stairs. But it was just Eddie saying he'd got him a something from the lunch hall. Kerr smiled. Eddie was the best mate he could ever hope for. It seemed crazy to think they'd once had a teacher-pupil relationship. Kerr couldn't imagine being friends with any of his students. But since starting work here, Eddie had taken Kerr under his wing, and Kerr honestly couldn't thank him enough.

Food and a chat with Eddie definitely helped a little, but the fact Jake hadn't even read the message by the end of lunch didn't fill Kerr with confidence.

Even come home time, there was nothing. Kerr walked back to Kirk Lane. The sun was still out, but it was a bit breezy. Thankfully, it wasn't too far as Kerr hadn't replaced his car since his old one had packed in. He had a bicycle, and both Eddie and his mum were awesome for giving lifts if he needed them, but really, he should get a new one.

He'd barely shrugged off his jacket in the hallway when his phone began to vibrate in his pocket.

Jake's name lit up the screen.

Kerr stared at it for a moment, a dull weight settling in his stomach.

He answered.

'Hey.'

'What the hell?' Jake's voice came through tight with fury. 'Georgie showed up at your house? Why?'

Kerr moved into the kitchen, switching on the kettle with his free hand. 'She literally just said she wanted to talk to you. That's all.'

'Talk to me?' Jake's laugh was brittle. 'About what? Has she lost the plot? Does she think now that her tennis career is over she can call me up and we'll start over?'

'I... um.' Kerr rubbed his forehead. Why hadn't he thought of that? Was that what she wanted? 'She didn't say anything like that.'

'*This. Is. The. Pits.*' The words were clipped. 'What the hell was she thinking? Turning up out of nowhere like that?'

Kerr leaned against the counter, listening to the kettle begin to rumble. 'I don't get it either.' He wasn't going to admit he'd watched her retirement interview and heard the quip about her buying a campervan. It had seemed like a joke at the time, but here she was... in a campervan. Kerr didn't understand. He didn't need to know. And he definitely wouldn't confess that he'd ever watched her on TV – even if he had. Many times – and absolutely not to Jake.

'God, the nerve of her.' Jake's voice had shifted from angry to something rawer, more wounded. 'I've built a life. A good one. With someone who actually gives a toss.'

The kettle clicked off, but Kerr didn't move to make his tea. 'I know, Jake.'

'Well, don't tell her how to contact me. Don't give her my number. Don't tell her anything about me. Nothing. I mean it,' Jake insisted. 'She doesn't get to walk back into my life when it suits her. Not after what she did. I don't want to speak to her. I want nothing to do with her. And make it quite clear that she stays away from me and my family. She's not welcome.'

'Yeah, ok. Sure. I understand.'

'Good,' Jake said. 'Thanks for having my back on this.'

After they hung up, Kerr stood in his kitchen, staring at the neglected mug and tea bag.

Why did he get the feeling that even if he told Georgie all that, this was far from over?

Chapter Five

Georgie

Georgie tugged her sunglasses down as she wandered down Glenbriar High Street. A sense that people were watching her was nothing new. She'd spent her life being public property. But this was different. She half-expected people to stop and say something. Perhaps ask if she was actually Georgie Porter, or if she was back in Glenbriar for good. But so far no one had. A few eyes had turned her way, but that was it. And she shouldn't complain. It was better than having her privacy invaded by a bunch of strangers.

The September sun was bright and warmed her shoulders through her oatmeal jumper. The street felt both familiar and strangely foreign. It had always been a popular little town, but now it looked even more artisan with lots of cafes and independent stores.

She peered in the windows of a few places. In Wood 'n' Chic – an upcycled furniture store with a really beautiful window display full of gorgeous pieces, a woman with burgundy hair, multiple ear piercings and a studded brow was setting up a display on a dresser painted in duck-egg blue.

Further down was a smartly done up hair salon called Cutting Edge. Georgie fancied having something done to her hair. Even just a couple of days in a campervan had made it feel a bit brittle. Maybe they could fit her in somewhere for a wash and blow dry. She pushed open the door and went in. Her gaze fell instantly on a face she recognised. Hayley McBride. She was laughing as she cut a client's hair. At school, she and Georgie had been friends. Hayley was one of the nicest people around, and Georgie's insides did a little flip. Would Hayley be pleased to see her? Or was this going to be hard work? After all, Georgie hadn't kept in touch. And for all she knew, Hayley might have heard what she did to Jake and be angry with her.

A young woman approached to speak to Georgie, but at that moment, Hayley glanced around. Her scissors froze mid-air.

'Oh, my goodness.' Hayley's eyes widened. 'Georgie Porter?'

Georgie pushed her sunglasses up onto her head. 'Yeah... it's me. Surprise?'

Hayley leaned in and whispered something to her client.

'How can I help you?' the young assistant asked.

'I'm looking for a wash and style. Sometime this week.'

The assistant sat behind the counter and looked at a screen.

'Well, hello you.' Hayley tapped Georgie on the shoulder.

'Hi.' Georgie gave her a weak smile.

Three seconds of silence followed. Then Hayley let out a delighted squeal and enveloped Georgie in a hug. 'What are you doing here?' Hayley pulled back to look at her. 'I never thought we'd see you in Glenbriar again.'

Georgie's chest filled with warmth, and she smiled. 'It was a bit last-minute. I'm just passing through, really. For a few days, maybe a week. I have a campervan.'

'Well, that I need to see,' Hayley gestured to her client, a woman with light brown hair, who was watching Georgie with unconcealed interest. 'I need to finish my client's hair, but I'd love to catch up while you're here.'

'Are you friends?' Hayley's client asked. 'I mean…' She put her hand on her chest. 'I am your biggest fan. That backhand in the Wimbledon quarterfinals three years ago, was it? I screamed so loud my husband thought I was being murdered.'

A mixture of pleasure and awkwardness that came with being recognised washed through her. 'That's very kind.'

'I can't believe Georgie Porter is here. Hayley, you never said you were friends with tennis royalty!'

'We go back to primary school,' Hayley said.

'I'm Amanda Reid,' Hayley's client said, almost as though she expected Georgie to know her. 'I'm the chairperson of the Glenbriar Tennis Club. Nothing fancy like what you're used to, but we're passionate.'

'That's where it all started for me.' Georgie's mind wandered back to those simpler days. She'd always had fun at that club.

'Actually—' Amanda narrowed her eyes. 'You must know Elise. Elise Reid? She's your friend, isn't she?' She looked at Hayley.

Georgie nodded. 'Yes, I remember Elise.'

'She's my sister-in-law. I'm married to her brother.'

'Small world,' Georgie murmured. Or maybe just small-town syndrome. While some of it was a little awkward and not what she was used to, another part of it was rather comforting.

'And Genevieve married my brother,' Hayley said, alluding to one of their other friends.

'Oh really? Wow...' Georgie tried to put together all the missing pieces.

'How are they? Elise and Genevieve.'

'Great,' Hayley said.

'Elise is back living in Glenbriar now,' Amanda added. 'She works for a tour company. If you're still here at the weekend, you should come to our open day. She'll be there. The club would lose their minds if you showed up. It would be amazing.'

Georgie blinked and sucked on her lip. 'Oh, that's really kind, but I'm not sure how long I'll be around.'

'Well, if you are, please don't be a stranger,' Amanda said brightly. 'You'll always be welcome. You're like our patron saint.'

Hayley caught Georgie's eye, and they smiled at each other.

'Um, I can get Hayley to do your hair tomorrow, if you want?' the assistant put in.

'Perfect, thanks.' Georgie gave her details, then looked back at Hayley, who had resumed cutting Amanda's hair. 'I'll see you tomorrow then.'

'See you.' Hayley waved to her.

'And I hope to see you at the club,' Amanda added.

Georgie left, unable to stop smiling. An undercurrent of uncertainty flowed through everything she did right now, but the thought of reconnecting with friends boosted her spirits as she carried on around the town.

After buying some supplies, she returned to Ayu – or maybe she should call her Snon... S̲till-n̲o-N̲ame – and headed back to Heather Glen.

It was such a beautiful place. Almost as soon as she was back, she settled into a folding chair positioned to face the stream. It burbled through the trees in harmony with the chirping birds. No screaming fans. No cameras. No coaches analysing her stance or agents scheduling her time in fifteen-minute increments.

Just peace. Perfect peace.

She closed her eyes, letting herself embrace it, not allowing any thoughts to permeate her mind.

'I could get used to this,' she murmured to no one.

The morning's encounter with Hayley and Amanda pushed into her mind, and she allowed it. It was a happy thought. Perhaps coming to Glenbriar wasn't a mistake after all. Perhaps she could find some peace here, even if only for a few days. Even if—

Her thoughts snagged on the real reason she'd come. Jake.

Her eyes opened, and she got to her feet. She didn't want that thought.

Returning to the van, she changed into her running gear and headed off around the loch. She wasn't as fast as she used to be, but she could still do this circuit in a good time if she pushed herself.

Her feet pounded the ground as she took the track up a hill and then down again through the woods. The path curved and narrowed, dappled light flickering through the canopy above. Birds chirped. Her breath sawed in and out of her chest.

The burn in her legs was welcome. She pushed harder, her stride lengthening, the ache growing with each rise. Her lungs protested, her ponytail bounced with every step, and sweat trickled down the back of her neck.

No one could catch her here.

She turned onto the home stretch – an open track that skirted the water's edge, then climbed a sharp rise before she descended into the campsite. The wind picked up and cooled her burning cheeks, but her crop top clung to her skin, and her chest heaved with each breath.

By the time she reached the campervan, her legs were jelly and her heart thundered like a drum. She bent over, hands on her knees, dripping sweat onto the ground.

'Bloody hell,' she muttered to herself, straightening with effort. 'Still got it... just.'

She fumbled with the door, her hand slick on the handle, and climbed inside. The air was warm and stuffy. Her trainers scuffed against the mat as she kicked them off and headed straight to the little fridge.

She pulled out a bottle of water, twisted off the lid, and gulped half of it in seconds, the cool liquid trickling down her throat. She leaned back against the counter, still catching her breath.

A knock came on her door, and she jumped. Who the hell? Maybe Logan, the owner, wanted something? Hopefully not a nosy fan who'd seen her running. Could she tiptoe to the window and try to see? Or would it be too obvious?

'Hello,' came a man's voice. It could be Logan, but she wasn't sure. 'Georgie? Are you in there?'

Wait a moment... Was that Kerr?

She pulled open the door with her sweaty palms.

Kerr, in a dark grey hoodie and jeans, took a half-step back as the door swung open. His gaze flicked over the sweaty hair stuck to her neck, her flushed cheeks, her damp vest top clinging to her.

Georgie crossed her arms, hyperaware of the state she was in.

'Sorry,' she said, breath still ragged. 'I'm just back from a run.'

'Yeah, I can see that.' His lips twitched, but not in a smile.

She waited. He didn't move.

'I tried to call.' He rubbed his hand over the back of his neck. 'The number you gave me – I think it's missing a digit or something. It wouldn't connect.'

Georgie frowned. 'Oh.' Her head drooped. 'I must've... I didn't mean to mess you about. Sorry.'

'Well...' His jaw tensed, and he looked at her squarely. 'I have a message from Jake.'

Her stomach dropped. She gripped the edge of the door tighter, bracing herself.

'He doesn't want to see you.'

He said it gently, but it still hit like a punch to the chest.

'I... What?'

Kerr held her gaze. 'I'm just the messenger. Jake was clear. He's not ready, and he doesn't think seeing you would help him. I'm sorry.'

She stared at him. Her throat tightened, but she refused to let her emotions show. She was well practised at this game – just like being on court.

'Right.' She nodded slowly. 'Ok.'

'I didn't come here to upset you.' A crease appeared between his brows. 'You were the one who wanted this.'

Their eyes met again, and in that brief moment, heat burned inside her. Yes. She wanted it.

'Well... yeah. Thank you for delivering the message. And coming all the way out here to do it.'

'No worries.' The ghost of a smile touched his lips. Then he turned and walked away, his tall figure receding down the path towards the car park.

Georgie watched until he disappeared around the bend, the crunch of his footsteps fading away. Beyond the gravel track, the trees lining the edge of the campsite stood ablaze with colour, their russet and gold leaves shifting in the breeze and drifting gently to the ground. Somewhere nearby, a bird called before silence returned. She closed the door with a soft click. The campervan, so cosy and comforting just minutes ago, now felt confining. She sank back into her chair and put her head in her hands.

What now?

The practical part of her brain suggested the obvious: pack up, drive away, find a new destination. Or go back to London... and do whatever.

Except... except she had a strange feeling that something was still unfinished. Not with Jake, but with herself. With Glenbriar.

Georgie took a deep breath. She'd left this place long ago in search of a different life.

Maybe this time, she could give it a real chance.

Even if only for a little while.

CHAPTER SIX

Kerr

Eddie was bouncing higher than the tennis balls, nodding enthusiastically to everyone who passed.

'Great weather, isn't it?' He clapped Kerr's shoulder. 'Perfect day for this.'

'Mmm,' Kerr agreed, watching a couple of people warming up. 'Amanda isn't best pleased that I haven't found a new partner for the mixed doubles. Bit rich coming from her. She's the one who drove Antonia away.'

Eddie frowned, though he still seemed to be twinkling behind it. 'Yes, I'm sorry Antonia left.' He glanced around and lowered his voice. 'We both know what Amanda can be like.'

There was no denying that. She was a control freak – and that was putting it mildly.

'But in this case, I don't think there was any unpleasantness. Amanda is a very kind woman and usually has people's best interests at heart. She just takes a bit of getting used to. I might give Antonia a call and see if she's up for coming back at some point. Maybe now things have died down a bit.'

'Good idea.' Kerr screwed up his face. 'But it doesn't help me find a partner for today and, of course, with Amanda being Amanda, she's already made up the rota, so if I pull out, it messes everything up.'

'Hmm, yes.' Eddie scanned around as if looking for some unsuspecting woman he could pounce on and beg to partner Kerr. Eddie was such a charmer Kerr wouldn't put it past him to succeed. 'Hold on a second.' Eddie's voice cut across Kerr's thoughts. 'Isn't that...?'

Kerr followed his gaze. Near the clubhouse, Amanda was standing with a tall, slim woman in oversized sunglasses, a short white tennis dress and zipped up jacket. Her dark hair was pulled back in a plait that draped over one shoulder. She tilted her head, laughing at something Amanda had said.

It was Georgie.

'Bloody hell,' Kerr muttered.

'Indeed,' Eddie said.

'What's she doing here?' Kerr watched as Amanda launched into an enthusiastic chat, complete with hand gestures.

'I thought you said she'd gone.' Eddie squinted into the sun. 'Didn't you tell her Jake didn't want to talk?'

'I did.' Kerr plucked his racquet strings.

'Maybe she's just here for the cakes. Amanda has gone all out with that traybake table.' Eddie said it with a grin, but he put his arm around Kerr's back and patted his shoulder. 'Or maybe she's changed her mind about leaving.'

Kerr didn't answer. Georgie turned slightly. She hadn't seen them yet – or if she had, she was doing a cracking job of ignoring them.

'I don't suppose she knows you're a member here,' Eddie said.

'Why would she even care?' Kerr threw out his hands. 'She doesn't know anything about me.'

'I'll see if I can find out what's going on from Amanda.' Eddie tapped the side of his nose. He was the brave man who partnered Amanda for the mixed event.

'Uh-oh,' Kerr muttered.

Eddie followed his line of sight, then winced in sympathy. Amanda was bearing down on them like a woman on a mission, Georgie in tow.

'Kerr, Eddie.' Amanda beamed. 'Look who's here. Isn't this wonderful?'

Kerr kept his expression neutral, though his jaw tightened. Georgie hovered a pace behind Amanda, fiddling with her racquet. She glanced at Kerr, then away again, as if fascinated by the autumn colours on the trees outside the court.

'This is Georgie Porter.' Amanda gestured to her. 'The one and only. Did you know she started out on these very courts?'

'Indeed, I do,' Eddie said warmly. 'I used to teach Georgie.'

Georgie smiled. 'Oh, yeah. You're Mr Caldwell.'

'Call me Eddie. You're not at school anymore.'

'I think Eddie has taught almost everyone in the town at some point,' Amanda said. 'And this is Kerr.'

Kerr gave a curt nod. 'Yeah, we've met.'

'Oh, you have, have you?' Amanda clapped her hands. 'Well, that makes everything simpler and so much better because Georgie has very kindly agreed to step in for Antonia in the mixed doubles. You're saved, Kerr – and I don't have to redraw the rota.'

'Right.' Kerr exchanged the tiniest tight-lipped look with Eddie.

Georgie's eyebrows lifted, a flicker of confusion crossing her face. 'I didn't realise...'

'Isn't it perfect?' Amanda continued. 'Well, it is for you, Kerr. You'll be unbeatable with Georgie as your partner.'

'Um...' Kerr opened his mouth, but Amanda was already talking again.

'It's a complete win-win. Now, Eddie, come on – we need a quick practice before we start. We'll leave you two to discuss tactics.'

Before Eddie could so much as blink, Amanda looped her arm through his and steered him off towards the nearest court. He shot Kerr a helpless look over his shoulder.

Kerr looked at Georgie. Georgie looked at the ground.

Brilliant.

Kerr's hands felt oddly disconnected from his body as he shifted his feet. 'I thought you'd be long gone from Glenbriar by now.'

Georgie adjusted her plait. 'Just... taking some time to relax.' Her eyes met his briefly, then darted away. 'The tennis club seemed like a good place to start.'

'Right.'

'I didn't know you'd be here. And when Amanda asked me to step in, she didn't say who with.'

'Would it have made a difference?'

She gave a little shrug. 'Probably. I'm not sure this is ideal for either of us.'

Kerr let out a sigh. 'It's fine. It's just tennis.'

Just tennis with the woman who'd broken his brother's heart. Just tennis with the woman he'd wished had chosen him and not Jake.

'Exactly.' Georgie tightened her plait and adjusted her sweatbands like she was on Centre Court and not court two of the lowly Glenbriar Tennis Club.

'Shall we have a knock up, then?' He took a ball from his pocket and bounced it. He knew she would wipe the floor with him.

'Sure, why not?'

They hit a few balls back and forth. The bounce was high on the hard-court surface. Georgie moved lightly, her shots easy and clean, but she wasn't going full pelt. Not even close.

She was going easy on him.

Kerr gritted his teeth and sent back a sharper shot than necessary.

With someone else, he might make a witty remark – something about her letting him win or accusing her of being secretly bionic – but the words stuck. Banter didn't feel right for so many reasons. His limbs tensed.

Georgie whipped back her racquet and slapped the ball, sending it whipping past him. He didn't even try to reach it, just bounced the ball again, jaw tight, trying to quiet the frustration buzzing in his chest.

Across the courts, Amanda's voice rang out like a starting pistol. 'Let's get going, folks! First matches are friendlies, so no pressure. Visitors and new members – come and get involved!'

'That's us.' Kerr headed towards the baseline. Georgie jogged around and joined him. 'You serving or me?'

'I don't mind.'

He shrugged. 'You go, then. Show us what you're made of.'

She gave him a half smile.

Amanda and Eddie took their places on the far side. Amanda was practically vibrating with competitive energy while Eddie gave Kerr a quick grin and a wink before turning to face Georgie's serve.

The first rally was short – Amanda netted the return – but the second went long, a fast-paced back and forth that ended with Kerr catching the very edge of the tramline.

'Brilliant!' Georgie thrust her hand up.

Without thinking, Kerr reached to meet it in a high-five. Their palms smacked together with a satisfying crack.

And instantly, he regretted it.

He was meant to dislike her on Jake's behalf. Not enjoy playing with her. Not be thinking about her in any way other than as his brother's ex. But she was easy to play with – quick, intuitive, almost instinctively in sync with his movements. Electricity seemed to buzz around her as she moved, her ponytail swinging, legs long and powerful beneath her skirt.

Every so often, she flashed him a grin, flushed and breathless, and something traitorous stirred in his chest.

Kerr flexed his hand as they changed ends, trying to shake off the awareness prickling at the edges of his focus. He was supposed to keep a cool head. But hell, she was magnetic when she was in her element, and despite himself, he was starting to enjoy this.

She gave him another look, and he held it for a beat too long.

No way could she know everything that she stirred in his head or heart. And why should she care? She probably had thousands of admirers worldwide. Kerr was no different.

After another couple of games, the match ended.

'You two were brilliant.' Eddie bounded over, slinging an arm around Kerr's shoulder. 'Absolutely brilliant. The dynamic duo of Glenbriar.' He pulled Kerr into a man hug and whispered in his ear. 'And you survived. Well done.' He clapped Kerr's back.

'Thanks, man.'

'Yes, you were wonderful.' Amanda looked slightly displeased at being beaten. 'That's my husband and children arriving. I should go and see them. Oh, and Georgie, come with me and I'll reintroduce you to Elise. She's dying to see you.'

Georgie glanced at Kerr, then put out her hand. 'Well played,' she said.

He took her hand and shook it. She held on a little longer than expected, and Kerr held his breath. 'You too.'

'Let's get a drink,' Eddie murmured.

The clubhouse patio hummed with post-match chatter, tennis bags slumped against chair legs like exhausted spectators. Kerr nursed a pear and ginger cooler – the taste fitting for the autumnal afternoon – trying to ignore the way his body still buzzed from the match. From playing with *her*.

'I doubt she'll stick around.' Eddie screwed up his eyes at his drink like he hadn't expected it to be so sharp. 'So don't worry too much.'

'It just hacks me off that she's here at all.'

'Hopefully, she'll leave after this.' Eddie knocked back his drink with a shudder. 'Oh lord, here comes Amanda again. What does she want now?'

Georgie was following her. 'Oh hell.' Kerr tried to turn away, but it was too late.

'You two were fantastic out there.' Amanda beamed, looking between Kerr and Georgie. 'I had a feeling you'd play well together.'

'Just lucky,' Kerr muttered.

Amanda clasped her hands together. 'Now, Eddie, Kerr, do you remember the meeting I told you about next Saturday in Glasgow? About the MUGA fundraising initiative?'

'Um, yeah.' Kerr rubbed the back of his neck. He had a habit of signing up for things like this, then forgetting all about them. Hopefully, it wouldn't interfere with helping the local band at the Autumn Gold Festival. Community events were great, but maybe he'd taken on too much.

'We've been shortlisted for the community funding grant.' Amanda's voice dropped as if sharing state secrets. 'And someone really should go to that meeting. It doesn't look good if we don't have a representative.'

'Aren't you going?'

'I can't. Too much on with the kids. Are either of you free?' She looked hopefully at them. 'As schoolteachers, you'd be able to talk all about the importance of the MUGA for young people.'

'I'm afraid I can't,' Eddie said. 'It's my partner's birthday, and he'd never forgive me if I missed it for a MUGA meeting.'

'Ah, of course.' Her eyes landed on Kerr.

Kerr gave a shrug. 'I don't have a car at the moment.'

'What about the train?' Amanda smiled.

'I could do it,' Georgie said.

Three heads turned to her.

'I've got the campervan.' She fiddled with the lid of her water bottle. 'I don't know much about the funding, but it sounds like the sort of thing I'd like to be involved in.'

Kerr stared at her, torn between gratitude for the potential escape route she'd just offered and annoyance at the thought of her muscling in after being back all of five minutes.

'I mean, I like promoting sport for young people, though I don't know enough about the club's history or the application process.' She shrugged.

Amanda clapped her hands together. 'You would be ideal. The perfect ambassador. But I understand your misgivings. How about you both go together? Kerr knows the history, you can drive the van. And with you there, I don't think any committee would say no.'

'I'm not sure—' Kerr started.

'It makes perfect sense, doesn't it?' Amanda looked at Eddie.

'Only if they both agree to it.'

Amanda looked at them both, one by one, as though she couldn't understand any possible objections. And objectively, there shouldn't be any. She was right. It could be ideal. Only it meant being stuck with Georgie for the day.

Kerr sighed, feeling cornered, options disappearing faster than one of Georgie's serves. He looked at Georgie. She also looked mortified at this turn of events.

But it was just one day. And for a good cause.

'Um... Yeah. Ok,' Kerr said.

'And you, Georgie?' Eddie asked.

'Sure.' She gave a tight smile.

'So that's settled,' Amanda said. 'I'll email you both the application details and the meeting location.' She checked her watch. 'Oh! I need to announce the next round.'

She bustled away before either of them could respond, leaving an awkward silence in her wake.

'Sorry,' Georgie said after a moment. 'I was trying to help, not hijack things. I might have put my foot in it again... Not for the first time.' She looked down at her shoes.

Kerr sighed, running a hand through his hair. 'No worries.' He shared a glance with Eddie, then poured himself another drink. He might need something a lot stronger than that to get through the meeting.

Eddie patted his back. 'I'm sure you two will have wonderful results if your on-court performance was anything to go by.'

With a raised eyebrow, Kerr stared at him, but Eddie winked. Kerr's eyes returned to Georgie, and she gave him a very faint smile.

What had he got himself into?

Chapter Seven

Georgie

'It's just a meeting,' Georgie told her reflection. 'Not Wimbledon.'

But it didn't feel that simple. Driving Kerr to Glasgow was going to be a special kind of torture – one she'd freely signed up for. Her motives had felt charitable at the time, but she wouldn't deny she had her own agenda. Nothing harmful. But this was a chance. With barely an idea of what she wanted to do with her career, it made sense to find out new opportunities. Especially in sport. This meeting would interest her.

The kettle clicked off, and Georgie made a green tea. Perhaps today would be the perfect chance to clear the air with Kerr, though she wasn't sure she wanted to open up that can of worms. Maybe leaving their messy history firmly in the past was the most sensible course of action, but it was weird just ignoring it. Still, it wasn't like she planned to stick around. So getting through one day shouldn't really be a big deal.

'Approach it like a match,' she told herself. Though maybe treating Kerr like an opponent wasn't a good idea either.

After she'd finished her breakfast, she dressed in navy tapered trousers and an oatmeal merino jumper. She didn't want to wear too much make-up, but campervan living was making her feel a lot less polished than usual, so she spent a fair amount of time putting on her barely-there foundation, a dab of tinted lip balm, and a sweep of mascara.

She twisted her hair into a ponytail.

She was picking Kerr up at seven – even though he'd seemed sceptical about the need to leave so early. What would he think when she told him she wanted to go via the back roads? The motorways around Glasgow looked scary, and she'd found a route on the satnav that showed what looked like a fairly decent route through the Trossachs.

Outside, the morning looked unspectacular and a little overcast. The wind teased the trees, and autumn leaves fluttered down like snow; it had an oddly familiar, homely feel about it. A far cry from the tennis resorts of the last thirteen years.

Did she miss them?

She wasn't really sure how she felt about any of it. Everything had a similar sense of being temporary and transient. And while that was freeing in some ways, it also left a hollowness.

The track through the campsite was empty this early on a Saturday morning, and she rolled the van out of the gates and headed into Glenbriar. Hardly anyone was in the main street either. The corner that led up the hill to Kirk Lane was a little tight in the van with the row of parked cars down one side, but she got by without any mishap and pulled up outside the little house where she'd come just the other day looking for Jake.

Kerr emerged looking like he'd stepped out of an advert for menswear. His charcoal jumper sat perfectly over a collared black shirt, showing off his broad shoulders, and his dark jeans hugged a trim waist and long legs. He was tall and strong, and while he'd looked athletic in his tennis gear, he looked equally good in casual wear.

Georgie opened the window. 'Morning.'

'Hi.' Kerr slung a jacket over his arm and gave her a vague little smile as he headed around to the passenger side of the van.

'So, how are you today?' she asked.

'Fine.' He put a backpack on the floor at his feet. 'You?'

'Yeah, I'm good.' She adjusted the extendable arm on the window where she'd clipped her phone and checked it was still showing the route she'd picked. 'Hopefully it'll be a useful meeting.'

Kerr leaned on the windowsill but turned slightly to look at her, raking his hand through his dark hair, which had some length at the sides and back, but still looked well kept and tidy. Objectively he was very handsome, even if she really shouldn't notice or care. 'If it's not, I can see Amanda being unimpressed. She seems to think you're a trump card or something.'

'Yeah.' Georgie pulled off. 'I mean... Well, part of me hopes I can help get the funding she wants, but I guess the other part of me worries that if we do, it'll only be because of...' She cringed.

Whatever she said here was going to sound like she was beefing herself up.

'Who you are,' Kerr finished before she could come up with a better way to phrase it.

'Well... Yes. I don't think that *should* be the case. It should be on merit.'

'Of course it should, but I suppose Amanda hopes the committee are as starstruck as she is.'

Georgie narrowed her eyes and huffed. 'I hope you're not going to use this trip to be mean to me.'

'Why would I be? And was that mean to you? It was possibly a bit mean to Amanda, but it's also true.'

Georgie drove on. She had to join the main road for a short while, but it wasn't a motorway and this early on, it was still quiet; traffic was picking up steadily. The satnav showed her a turnoff in a few miles that would take her cross-country to a town called Crieff, and from there the road would lead to the Trossachs. Flipping on the indicator, she moved into the exit lane.

'Where are you going?' Kerr asked.

'I don't like driving on the motorways in the van,' she said. 'There's a lovely back road that we can go on.'

Kerr stared at her. 'A back road? All the way to Glasgow?'

'Yeah. I've mapped it out on my phone. It's not *that* much longer, timewise,' she said.

'Assuming the roads are free of tractors, log trucks and other slow-moving vehicles. Why can't you just take the main road? Not all of it is motorway. Some of it's just dual carriageway.'

'I prefer not to.'

He didn't argue, but he tapped a restless rhythm against his thigh. Georgie kept her eyes firmly on the road ahead, pretending not to notice.

Silence stretched between them as she steered the van down the twisty road next to a large expanse of fields. Harvesters were out in some of them. Others had bales piled high, and some were home to sheep or cows. All of it very pretty, but none of it very fast.

Kerr let out a sigh. 'How much longer does this route add?'

'Not much.' She focused on a bend in the road. 'Maybe fifteen minutes?'

He made a noncommittal sound that suggested he didn't believe her.

'The van gets a bit... overwhelmed on motorways.'

'The van does?'

She caught his raised eyebrow, and a warm flush crept up her neck. 'Fine. I get overwhelmed. Happy?'

'I didn't say anything.' But his posture relaxed slightly.

Georgie drummed her fingers on the steering wheel. 'I haven't been driving long. I only got my license a couple of years ago. I don't like driving fast, so country roads are better for both of us.'

Kerr shifted in his seat. 'I wouldn't have thought it would be a problem for you. Playing tennis in front of huge crowds must be pretty scary. And you did that. Is driving worse than that?'

'There's considerably less danger of death.'

'I suppose, though I know which one I'd rather do.' He checked his watch again. 'It's quarter to eight. It starts at nine thirty. I'm not sure we'll get there in time.'

'We'll make it.'

The van chose that moment to make a concerning rattling sound, like someone had filled a tin can with loose bolts and shaken it vigorously. Kerr's head snapped towards the dashboard.

'What was that?'

'Something in the glove box.' At least, she hoped it was.

Kerr glanced out the window, where clouds were gathering. 'Looks like rain coming. This road probably gets a lot of surface water, so it might be just as dangerous as the motorway.'

'You're not exactly helping, are you?' Georgie raised an eyebrow.

'Sorry.' He looked away but seemed to give a half laugh as he did.

They'd barely got five miles further when fat raindrops splatted against the windscreen. Georgie flicked on the wipers, which squeaked across the glass. The downpour intensified with alarming speed, drumming on the van's roof like impatient fingers. What had been clear visibility turned murky, the road ahead becoming a blurred grey ribbon.

Georgie's knuckles whitened on the steering wheel. She leaned forward slightly, squinting through the inadequately cleared windscreen. The wipers were fighting a losing battle, smearing rather than clearing the glass.

'Do you want me to—'

'I'm fine,' she cut him off. She didn't need to be rescued. She could do this. The same rain would be falling on the motorway, so her choice was still an improvement.

The rain hammered down harder, a proper Scottish downpour that seemed determined to drown them. The van's headlights barely cut through the grey curtain, and the narrow road felt slippery and treacherous.

Kerr didn't say anything else, but his tension mirrored hers in the way he balled his fists and seemed to be bracing himself.

Georgie slowed right down, creeping along as she squinted forward. The wipers continued their futile battle against the torrent. Georgie carried on following the roads the satnav on her phone was pointing her, reminding herself that each turnoff took them closer to their destination. Though they still seemed to be a long way off.

'You're doing fine,' Kerr said quietly, and she blinked, taken off guard. 'I think there's a roundabout near here. My dad used to bring us here for days out.'

Their eyes met briefly, and something passed between them – an acknowledgment, perhaps, that this was out of her comfort zone.

'The roundabout's just ahead.' She checked the phone. 'Second exit.'

The rain hammered down as they approached the junction. Georgie saw the roundabout through the curtain of water. No other cars were there, and the van lurched forward. 'Oops... sorry.'

Kerr didn't respond, still staring forward.

Georgie checked the time and the distance repeatedly. Forty minutes to cover twenty-six miles in this weather was going to be tight. Very tight.

Neither of them spoke for several minutes. The silence wasn't comfortable exactly, but Kerr seemed to have realised that fretting over the time wouldn't help – or improve the situation.

The windscreen wipers squeaked a melancholy rhythm. *Swish-squeak, swish-squeak,* the only sound apart from the rain and the rumble of the engine.

They passed through another village – stone houses tight to the roadside, a sleepy main street with a newsagent and a closed chippy. A dog trotted along the pavement beside its owner, oblivious to the rain. Georgie gritted her teeth as the van splashed through a shallow puddle that turned out to be deeper than it looked.

'We're getting there,' she muttered, mostly to herself.

Kerr leaned towards the satnav display on her phone. 'Still says twenty-five minutes.'

'That's better than an hour.'

'True, but it's taking us in at Milngavie. It'll be busier there.' He rubbed his thumb along his jaw. Georgie glanced sideways. His leg was bouncing.

'You're going to shake a hole in the floor at this rate.'

He let out a sharp breath that could have been a laugh. 'Sorry.'

'I said we'd get there,' she said. 'We *will* get there.'

The road curved through woodland, the trees bright even in this weather with their autumn colours beginning to show through.

A sign welcoming them to Milngavie appeared. Georgie exhaled. Not too far now. She swung the van through the roundabout, past a retail park with a supermarket and a café already busy with early morning customers.

'This is where the West Highland Way starts,' Kerr said. 'I always fancied doing it.'

'What is it?'

'A long-distance walk between here and Fort William. You either stop along the way in designated places or you camp.'

'Sounds fun.'

'Jake and I were going to do it, but... Well, other things happened.'

Was that a dig? Perhaps Jake had been so upset by the breakup he hadn't wanted to go with Kerr.

They both fell quiet again as the traffic thickened, brake lights flickering through the misty air. Georgie tightened her grip on the wheel and filtered onto the main road towards the city centre.

Her eyes flicked constantly between the signs, the satnav, and the clock.

The van crawled along, hemmed in by buses and taxis. Tower blocks loomed to one side, and the distant shape of the Hydro curved like a silver spaceship on the riverside.

'That's it up ahead.' Kerr pointed.

She nodded, shoulders easing a little. 'Finally.'

They were still a good five minutes away, even if the lights went in their favour. Which they wouldn't. Of course they wouldn't. The van jolted as she slowed for another red.

Finally, they reached the car park for the SECC. It was nine thirty-seven. Georgie cut the engine and unclipped her belt. 'We're only seven minutes late. They might not have started properly yet.' Though she knew this wasn't going to make a good impression.

Kerr didn't respond but took off his seatbelt and reached for his backpack. 'Let's go then. It's still quite a long way to the door.'

Georgie grabbed her bag.

They both stared at the downpour, which showed no signs of abating. The car park was a battlefield of puddles, some deep enough to qualify as small ponds.

Taking a deep breath, Georgie clutched her tote bag to her chest and pushed open the van door. The rain hit her like a cold shower, immediately finding every gap in her defences. She slammed the door shut and locked it with a quick press of the key fob, already feeling water seeping through her jacket.

They set off across the car park at a half-run, dodging the deeper puddles where possible. Georgie's white trainers were immediately marked with splashes of mud, and her carefully styled ponytail drooped under the assault.

Kerr headed towards a glass entrance about fifty meters away, where a canopy offered the promise of shelter.

They increased their pace, water splashing around them. Georgie's socks felt damp. Kerr's hair was plastered to his forehead.

They were almost there when Georgie's foot landed in a puddle deeper than it appeared, sending a spray of muddy water up her trouser leg. She stumbled, clutching her bag tighter.

'Oh, yuck,' she gasped. 'Look at my shoes.'

The white was now a mucky greyish brown.

'Maybe white shoes weren't the best idea.'

To her surprise, she started to laugh. Maybe it was hysteria, but she couldn't stop.

'What's so funny?'

'I'm not sure I even know.' She wiped rain or tears – it was impossible to tell – from her face. 'Look at us.'

Kerr's eyes travelled over her, and his expression cracked. The corner of his mouth twitched.

'We're going to look ridiculous,' he said.

They carried on up to the door. Georgie was still giggling, and as Kerr held open the door for her, she realised he was laughing too.

For that tiny moment, everything that had gone before was forgotten. But that was all about to change. They needed to find the meeting room and make sure they hadn't missed too much. Then they'd somehow have to act professionally while soaked to the skin... Was it appropriate to take off her shoes and tip them up? Georgie didn't imagine so. She'd survived several ice baths as a player, so surely a few hours in wet feet would be easy.

Chapter Eight

Kerr

Kerr made his way to the SECC reception area with Georgie, both of them dripping like they'd gone for a swim fully clothed. Once they were told which room to go to, they hurried down the corridor. The squeak of his wet boots on the polished floor announced their arrival more effectively than any entrance bell could have.

Heads turned as they entered, and Kerr's skin prickled with the special kind of embarrassment reserved for latecomers who interrupt meetings already in progress. He knew how annoyed he'd be if a student did this in class. Yet here he was doing exactly the same thing.

'Sorry we're late.' Kerr offered a sheepish smile.

A woman with cropped silver hair and electric-blue glasses rose from her seat at the head of the U-shaped table arrangement. Her smile was warm, her handshake firm.

'Don't worry,' she said. 'I'm Irene Tarrant, community development officer. We were just getting started. This weather is no friend to anyone.'

Kerr introduced himself. Beside him, Georgie extended her hand, her smile dazzling despite her bedraggled appearance.

'Georgie Porter, standing in for Amanda Reid.'

A ripple of chatter moved through the room, and Irene's eyes widened slightly with recognition. Perhaps Georgie would indeed ace this, like Amanda hoped.

'Well, we're delighted to have you both. Please grab some coffee and find seats.'

Kerr followed Georgie to the coffee station at the back of the room, hoping not to leave mucky footprints behind him. He poured black coffee into a paper cup.

They took seats at the table's far end, and Kerr pulled out his notebook – mercifully protected inside his waterproof backpack – and tried to catch up on what he'd missed.

A man in a polo shirt was walking through a PowerPoint presentation about funding streams and application deadlines. Kerr noted down key dates and information. The slides moved to examples of similar projects in other towns.

'The challenge for you all...' The presenter clicked to a new slide '...is demonstrating community engagement and sustainable usage. Without that, ScotActive Trust can't release the matched funding. We're very rigorous in the way we look at applications. Hopefully, today you'll get some idea of how viable your project is, and we'll be able to give you some pointers or let you know if you're on the right lines. As you all should be aware, no funding decisions will be made today, but we'll welcome discussions about various projects and hopefully when you leave you'll have a clearer idea on how to tailor your application in a way that will be mutually beneficial.'

Later, they broke into discussions around the table – people offering suggestions about usage surveys and letters of support from local clubs. Kerr listened, noting down which approaches might work best for Glenbriar.

'If I could ask something?' Georgie said.

All eyes turned to her.

'Would legacy arguments work here? Arguing the MUGA wouldn't just be about immediate usage but about creating pathways – showing how a facility like this turns recreational players into club members, club members into county players, and occasionally, county players into professionals. That was my route, after all.'

'Yes, there's no reason why not,' the presenter said. 'One of our main aims is to create a sporting future. So if you feel you can make this argument work on your behalf, then excellent.'

The room had gone quiet, everyone listening. Kerr watched with an odd sense of pride, almost like he was watching one of his pupils. Weird, really, but she seemed genuine in her desire for this project to succeed. Would she be around to see it to completion? Even if they secured the funding this year, it wouldn't exactly be built in a day.

As the morning progressed, Kerr couldn't keep his eyes off her. Was it just the media training kicking in and making her seem thoughtful, knowledgeable, and passionate about creating opportunities for others?

He'd assumed her presence on this project was a whim – another waystation on her campervan journey of self-discovery. But watching her discuss sporting infrastructure with the ScotActive Trust reps – who talked to her like the expert she was – gave Kerr a sense of empowerment. She knew her stuff, which meant he didn't feel out of his depth, or that he might not be able to bring about the outcome Amanda wanted. Georgie was the perfect person for this role.

By the time lunch break came around, Kerr was impressed, and less stressed. Partly because his clothes had almost dried, but mostly because of Georgie's input.

'Lunch is provided in the café,' Irene announced. 'We'll reconvene at one-fifteen to discuss the community consultation process.'

Kerr closed his notebook, catching Georgie's eye across the table. She raised an eyebrow. 'That was interesting, don't you think?'

'Yeah.' He gave a little nod. 'Let's get some lunch.'

The café hummed with the gentle clatter of cutlery and conversation, the scent of coffee and cooking making Kerr's stomach rumble. He leaned the flat of his palm against the counter, waiting for his turn to order, frowning at the display cabinet.

'Isn't there anything you like?' Georgie asked.

'What?' He met her gaze. Presumably she'd taken his less than delighted expression to be related to the food, but actually it was because of her. Maybe he should just straight up ask her why she was doing this. It was great to think an athlete like her would want to work with a community project, but Kerr had been programmed to look at her in a shady light since the Jake incident and couldn't help thinking she might have other motives. But what were they?

'Don't you like any of the sandwiches? They have soup and cooked things too.'

'I was just thinking. What are you having?'

'The soup sounds good. It'll warm me up a bit. My feet are so cold. I don't think my socks have dried properly yet.'

'Haven't you got other clothes in your van?'

'Yes. I might go and get some dry stuff. But what about you?'

'I think mine are dry.' He glanced at their feet. 'But my shoes are considerably thicker than yours.'

'True.'

They ordered food, and Kerr headed for a table while Georgie nipped off to get some dry socks from her van. Hopefully she would avoid the big puddle this time.

Kerr placed the wooden spoon with the number seven on it in the middle of the table and took a seat. Pulling out his phone, he scrolled through it, checking a string of messages from Eddie, and another from the Tavrach frontman, Adam Cormac, giving him some dates for the Autumn Gold Festival, and asking if Kerr was available to chat about what they needed him to do for them. Kerr thumbed out a reply, but before he'd hit send, a call came in. The name Jake flashing on the screen was unexpected. It wasn't like they never spoke, but they tended to message. Kerr's gut twisted as he hit the green accept button. Hopefully nothing was wrong.

He pressed accept, turning slightly towards the wall. 'Hey. Is everything ok?'

Jake's voice all but exploded through the speaker, loud enough that Kerr had to yank the phone away from his ear. 'What the hell is going on with Georgie?'

Kerr's pulse quickened. What did Jake mean? Kerr had nothing going on with Georgie. The fact she was here with him was almost a coincidence. And as for the past... Well, that was staying where it belonged.

'I don't know.' Which was true.

'Apparently, after she turned up on your doorstep looking for me, she didn't leave. I was chatting to Mum, and she told me lots of people have seen her. Mum works with someone we were at school with, and she said Georgie had been at the salon getting her hair done and making plans to meet someone at the tennis club. Do you still play there? Have you seen her there?'

Kerr pinched the bridge of his nose. Oh, the joys of the small-town gossip network.

'Yeah, she was at the tennis open day. I saw her there.'

'What the hell? What was she doing there?'

'Just revisiting her old stomping ground, I guess.' Though Kerr still wasn't completely sure himself.

'Did she speak to you?'

Kerr's insides contracted. Whatever he said here was going to incense Jake. If he told the truth and said yes, Jake would be livid. If he said no, Jake would be fuming that she'd blanked him – and that would also mean Kerr lying to his brother. Something he really didn't want to do. Not when he'd been harbouring secret feelings for Georgie for years that made him feel like he was living a lie every day.

'Yes, we spoke.'

'What did she say to you?'

'Well... we just talked about tennis really. My doubles partner dropped out, and the club chair thought it would be a good idea for Georgie to play with me. I didn't exactly have a choice.'

'Are you kidding me? And you're what, best mates now? Have you forgotten everything she did?'

Kerr leaned back in his seat, his free hand rubbing the tension building at the back of his neck.

'Of course I haven't,' he said. 'But I have to be civil.'

There was a weighted pause, and Kerr could almost see his brother's expression hardening. When he spoke again, Jake's voice was cold with disbelief.

'Civil? You know that she dumped me after I moved my whole life to be with her. And she didn't even tell me. I found out from the fucking TV like everyone else.'

'I remember.' Kerr closed his eyes briefly. This was exactly the conversation he'd hoped to avoid, especially here, especially now, with Georgie so close by. He'd spent years listening to Jake's anger and hurt, watching his brother rebuild himself after Georgie left. How could he tell Jake the woman who'd caused all this pain was with him at this very moment?

'I want to know what she's playing at,' Jake went on. 'Is she back in Glenbriar for good? Or just there to get some publicity, or what?'

'I'm not sure.' Kerr caught movement in his peripheral vision, someone approaching from behind. 'Listen, I—'

'I'm fizzing with her,' Jake snapped. 'She's got no right to do this. I thought she was gone for good.'

'She hasn't exactly done anything.'

'Apart from appearing on your doorstep. What kind of person would do that? It's out of order. It wouldn't surprise me if she tried to wheedle herself in with you. I get the feeling she's doing this to get at me. Have you seen her anywhere else other than at the club?'

Kerr's insides were knotted so tightly he almost felt like he couldn't eat that toastie he'd just ordered.

'Well, yes... Listen, I'm at the SECC at a meeting about funding for the MUGA.'

'What's that?'

'A multi-use games area. We're hoping to fundraise to get one put in near the tennis courts. Anyway... Amanda, the club chair, asked me to go and...' How could he say this? But was it any better not saying it and Jake somehow finding out down the line? 'So Georgie was asked to go too.'

'Are you saying she's in Glasgow with you right now?'

'Yes.' Kerr's focus was dragged away from the wall when he realised Georgie had returned and sat down opposite.

'Just the two of you?'

'Well, there are other people from other clubs, but from Glenbriar, yes.'

'Isn't that just great. Just like I said. She's worming her way back in.'

'Jake... I should go.' He tilted the phone away and muttered, 'She's right here, listening.'

'Give her a message from me then. She can go to hell.' The call ended, and Kerr stared at the phone, his jaw clenched tight enough to crack walnuts. Slowly, he raised his gaze and caught Georgie's eye.

Her face had gone blank, wiped clean of the animation that had lit it all morning, and her eyes were wide and cold. There was no question she'd heard Jake's final bitter words. Possibly more. The ambient noise of the café seemed to recede, leaving them in a bubble of awkward silence.

Great. Just great. Last week, everything had been normal. Now he was back in the wreckage of a Georgie Porter car crash. Why did she have to have this effect on him? And shouldn't he have grown out of it by now?

Chapter Nine

Georgie

The clatter of a tray being set down broke the silence spiralling out between Georgie and Kerr. A server placed her bowl of soup and a plate of toasties on the table, barely murmuring a word before disappearing. Georgie pulled the bowl towards her, warming her hands on it and breathing in the delicious lentil aroma.

She didn't ask who he'd been on the phone to. She didn't need to. She'd heard enough.

Kerr stared down at the toastie on his plate but didn't pick it up. The silence stretched. Georgie reached for her spoon and skimmed a layer of soup from the top.

'The, uh...' Kerr cleared his throat '...funding team seemed pretty positive this morning.'

'Mm.' She kept her eyes on her soup. Blew on it. Sipped. It scalded her tongue slightly, but at least it gave her an excuse not to speak.

'That legacy angle you brought up was a really good idea.' He pulled a corner from his toastie. 'I think it'll give the application a stronger case.'

Georgie set down her spoon carefully. 'Thanks.' She looked up, met his gaze. His eyes flicked away almost immediately, and he seemed to focus extra hard on slowly chewing his food.

'I guess you're used to giving speeches,' he said. 'Like after matches.'

She forced a small smile. 'Absolutely. It's compulsory, so I had to learn how to talk to the media. But you have to talk to classes every day, so you'll be just as used to it as me.'

'True.'

'Do the kids in your classes all behave?'

He cast her a faint huff of amusement, rubbing a hand over his stubbly jaw. 'Mostly, though there's always the odd one who causes trouble. Sadly, one troublemaker can dominate an otherwise pleasant class.'

'That must be annoying.'

'It can be frustrating.'

The quiet returned. The soup was too hot, and the tension was thicker than Kerr's doorstop toastie. Georgie's thoughts fluttered back to Jake and what she'd overheard. Her presence in Glenbriar was like a personal insult to him – even though he didn't even live there now.

The conversation about teaching had given her a fleeting window of opportunity – almost clarity. She knew nothing about the profession, but what if she went into coaching? She could return to the tour as a coach or even work at club level. Maybe even at her old club in Glenbriar.

'So,' she said eventually, 'if the funding is secured, can the MUGA be built straight away? Are all the plans in place?'

Kerr ran his fingers through his hair. 'Yeah, there are already plans. Ambitious ones too. Amanda thinks if we aim for the biggest and best, then even if we don't get all of it, we might at least get something.'

'What's ambitious about it?'

'It's not only the surface, but a cover, new changing room, and purpose-built storage area. It'll have extra lighting, so it can be used all year round at any time.'

'Sounds great.' Georgie had practised day in, day out as a child. The courts had floodlights for evening play, but in the rain it was miserable. If she did one thing before she left Glenbriar, it should be to make sure the MUGA got built. That was what her focus should be, to help build a lasting legacy in the town.

'Amanda's timeline is to have it ready for the summer next year. But it all depends on this funding.'

'Will you still be involved at that point?'

He nodded. 'Yeah. I plan to stay in Glenbriar for the long term. I think it's important to be involved in local initiatives.'

'Sounds good.' She would do the same. Only she didn't have anywhere local. Maybe she could tour around in the van and join committees in every town she rocked up at. Perhaps act like a travelling troubleshooter, going from place to place helping them set up sporting facilities, then moving on.

Across the table, Kerr shifted in his seat. 'Jake... didn't know you were here too. I'm sorry if you heard... anything.'

'I did.' She set down her spoon. 'I didn't come back to stir anything up. I did come looking for Jake, but only because I want to speak to him. To apologise.'

'If you want my advice, I'd steer well clear.' His voice was tight. 'Don't go poking about in the past. No good will come of it.'

Georgie nodded, and they fell silent again. He was probably right, but the idea of her history with Jake hanging about like a loose thread made her insides twist.

After lunch, they returned to the meeting room along with the others, the low hum of conversation fading as everyone found their seats. The presenter clicked on the laptop, and the projector screen lit up again.

'Right, welcome back, everyone. Hope you've had a chance to refuel. This next section is about making your application stand out to funders like ScotActive Trust. We'll be focusing on four key themes: community need, long-term impact, inclusivity, and working in partnership.'

Georgie uncapped her pen, already poised above her notebook. Next to her, Kerr rolled up his sleeves and leaned his forearms on the table, attention fixed on the screen.

The presenter advanced the slide. 'First off – community need. It's not enough to say you *want* a new facility. You have to show the gap. What's missing? Who's being left out? Where's the evidence?'

Georgie nodded slowly. She could already think of a few things and started jotting rough bullet points in the margin.

Community – that was an easy one. They could get local clubs involved. Netball, five-a-side, maybe even walking football. School groups too – primary and secondary. She tapped a finger lightly against her notebook, letting her pen hover.

Under sustainability, she scribbled: *eco surfacing, solar-powered lights, recycled materials?*

Accessibility – right, ramps for wheelchair users, maybe different height hoops for inclusive play. That blind netball team she'd seen online – there'd been a BBC feature. She could find the link, send it to Amanda.

She glanced towards Kerr again. He was watching the screen intently, but one knee bounced beneath the table. Either he was still tense from their conversation, or he just hated sitting still.

The presenter moved on, sharing examples of projects that had impressed funders before – a skatepark co-designed with local teenagers, a bowls club that opened its doors to dementia-friendly sessions. Georgie's brain whirred faster.

What if they ran open days? Taster sessions? Free beginner classes to encourage people who'd never tried a sport before? Maybe even a community coaching programme – train up volunteers, build skills locally, create something lasting.

She scrawled the ideas messily, almost illegibly, and underlined the whole lot twice. She couldn't undo the past, but maybe she could do this. Leave something behind in Glenbriar that was actually worth something.

Maybe even something that Kerr and his family would appreciate... Something better than the legacy her relationship with Jake had left.

When the meeting wrapped up, Irene bustled over and took Georgie's hand between both of hers. 'I can't let you go without saying how much I always admired you as a player. It's exciting to see you working with local groups like this. I'm sure with your skills, there would be national level jobs available to you if you were interested.'

'I... Well, I haven't really decided what I'll do yet.'

The warmth of Kerr's presence hovered just next to her, close enough that the scent of his spicy cologne stirred in the air between them. He was watching her, a steady heat radiating from his body. Her skin tingled in a way she hadn't expected.

'Keep it in mind,' Irene said. 'There are always roles in sport for achievers like you.'

Kerr hadn't said anything, but Georgie was convinced she'd heard the word 'favouritism' coming from him. It must have been telepathy or a guilty conscience, because his lips never moved. Nice lips they were too – not that she was looking.

'Ready?' Kerr asked.

Georgie nodded. 'I'll just nip to the loo before we go.'

When she returned from the toilets, Kerr was standing next to the glass doors in the lobby. Rain still lashed against them. The sky was a bruised grey colour.

Another dodgy drive was ahead. She almost wished she could hand over the keys to Kerr and ask him to drive. But would he want to? Who would in weather like this? And was he even insured to drive her car? She wasn't sure how that worked.

'Shall we run for it?' She glanced up at him. He was tall, over six foot and built as well as some of the guys on tour.

He nodded and pushed open the door into the downpour.

Georgie followed, the cold rain hitting her face like tiny needles. As water immediately began soaking through her flimsy jacket again, she thanked her lucky stars for having bought a van with good heating.

Ayu sat forlornly in the corner of the car park, looking less like a cheerful bohemian dream and more like a sodden, stranded lifeboat. Georgie fumbled in her pocket for the keys, fingers numb and clumsy from the cold.

'Come on, come on,' she muttered, finally extracting the keyring with its fluffy tennis ball charm, though it was now a sad, soaked thing that looked like it had been fished from a drain. Finally, she yanked the door open, and Kerr jumped in the passenger side, shaking himself like a dog. Georgie collapsed into the driver's side with an ungraceful squelch. Her navy trousers clung uncomfortably to her legs. She twisted her hair, wringing water onto the rubber floor mat.

'Well,' she said, 'at least we're consistent. Arrive drenched, leave drenched.'

Kerr wiped water from his face with the back of his hand. 'Do you have a towel or something?'

Georgie reached behind her seat, pulling out a small microfibre cloth – woefully inadequate for their current state, but better than nothing. She handed it to him. 'I've got better ones in the back if you want.'

'This is fine, thanks.' He rubbed at his hair.

'I'll get the heating on. It's good.' She turned the key in the ignition, and the van sputtered to life. She twisted the heating dial to maximum. Rain hammered on the roof, creating a deafening percussion. Georgie switched on the wipers, which barely cleared her view before fresh sheets of water obscured it again.

'I'd like to stop at the supermarket and get some food for when we get home,' Georgie said.

'Sure, but let's just take the main road this time, yeah?' Kerr frowned at her. 'It'll be quicker, and this weather isn't letting up.'

Georgie's hands tightened on the steering wheel. 'I'd rather stick to the back way,' she mumbled. 'I'm not happy driving on motorways in this weather.'

'Is it honestly worse than all those little twisty ones?'

'Yes. For me, it is.'

'Fine.' He leaned on the window. 'You're the driver.'

She pulled out of the parking space, windscreen wipers fighting a losing battle, and drove carefully to the exit, indicator ticking loudly.

Traffic out of the city was crawling. They edged through grid-locked junctions, brake lights glowing like a never-ending trail of fairy lights, only far less magical. The rain had eased to a miserable drizzle that clung to the windscreen like cling film smeared with grease no matter how fast the wipers flicked.

Georgie peered ahead at yet another sea of red lights.

Kerr tapped his phone screen. 'It's quarter past six. We've moved about three miles in the last half hour.'

'At this rate, we'll be back in Glenbriar sometime next week.'

'Don't tempt fate.'

They inched forward again. Georgie turned off the radio, which had been droning about disruption on the M8 for the past ten minutes. A man in a van next to them picked his nose with careless dedication.

'Attractive,' Kerr muttered.

'Really adds to the ambience.'

After more stop-starting for several minutes, they came to a supermarket. The car park was crammed with damp, glowering people pushing trolleys like they were crossing a battlefield.

'I'll come in too,' Kerr said as Georgie pulled into a somewhat tight space. 'I could do with getting a few things.'

'Ok.' She grabbed her tote bag from the footwell. 'Let's go.'

Once inside, they went their separate ways and Georgie raced around, grabbing what she needed. Kerr was already behind the tills with a carrier bag, waiting, when she got there.

Fifteen minutes later, they emerged and had another mad dash across the car park. Georgie tossed the stuff in the back, slammed the sliding door shut and climbed back behind the wheel.

'Look at this.' Kerr opened his bag. 'I bought some new socks.' He pulled out a twin pack of what looked like very thick and cosy ones. 'If we're going on a tour of the back roads, I want warm feet. I don't think they've recovered from this morning.'

'You should have bought pyjamas, then you could go and sleep in the back.'

'I did.'

'Are you serious?'

He snorted a laugh. 'Actually, yeah, but not for that reason. Just because they were on offer. I also got a couple of T-shirts from the same offer, plus shaving foam, a bag of rolls, some grapes and a tub of spreading cheese.'

'All very random.'

'Some of it I might have to eat soon. Depends on how long it takes us to get back.'

'That might be a while yet.'

They joined the slow queue to leave the car park. A group of seagulls fought over a chip bag outside the entrance, and a man was yelling at a trolley that wouldn't unlock.

By the time they'd finally turned off onto the back road, the sky had deepened to a moody charcoal and the van's headlights bounced off wet tarmac.

'My god, it's ten to seven.' Georgie tapped the wheel. They'd left at five.

'Two hours to travel less than twenty miles. Quality progress.'

'To be fair, we wouldn't have got much further on the motorway, would we?'

'Possibly not.' He smirked faintly and opened his bag of rolls. 'Do you want a roll with cheese spread?'

'I might give that a miss.'

The wipers dragged across the windscreen with a mournful *squeak-thump, squeak-thump*. Rain transformed the country road into a treacherous stream, water pooling at the edges and rushing in rivulets across the tarmac.

Georgie leaned forward in her seat, eyes narrowed against the gloom. Her knuckles were white on the steering wheel. A bend approached, and she slowed even further, taking it with painful caution. In her mind's eye, she thought she sensed Kerr's irritation building, though he didn't say anything and seemed relaxed enough, eating his rolls. Maybe it was her own inner critic that was frustrated at the turn of events, not the man beside her. At least he couldn't see the tight band of anxiety squeezing her chest.

A truck approached from the opposite direction, its headlights creating momentary blindness through the rain-streaked windscreen. Georgie held her breath as it passed, spraying a wave of water over the van that sounded like gravel hitting the metal.

'You ok?' Kerr asked.

'Fine,' she said automatically, though it was a total lie. This was like a living nightmare. 'Just concentrating.'

He nodded, and another silence descended, punctuated only by the relentless percussion of rain and the squeaky wipers.

'We could pull over until it eases,' Kerr suggested.

'I've got it,' she insisted. 'I mean, it might not stop all night.'

If she was on her own, she'd put on one of her audiobooks, but the last one she'd listened to was not something she wanted to share with Kerr. Hearing spicy scenes about characters forced into an only one bed situation and using it for their mutual pleasure was probably not the kind of thing she needed to share with Kerr right now. Though the thought made her snigger.

'What's so funny?' Kerr asked.

'Oh... um... nothing. Just thinking.'

The scene that was now unfolding in her mind, however, was absolutely not something she was prepared to reveal to him.

CHAPTER TEN

Kerr

A gust of wind caught them broadside, pushing the campervan towards the verge before Georgie corrected it with a quick twist of the wheel.

'Christ.' Kerr grabbed the edge of his seat.

He hadn't meant to say anything, but it was reflex. Georgie's small frown told him she wasn't impressed.

'Sorry,' she said.

'No need to be sorry.' Kerr gave her arm a very gentle pat. 'It's this wind. It's not good.'

'Did you see this on the weather forecast?' Georgie's eyes flickered momentarily to where he'd touched her arm, before she returned to squinting through the windscreen. 'It's getting proper wild.'

Kerr's stomach rolled as they hit a pothole, and he swallowed hard, fighting the sickly sensation crawling up his throat. He hadn't suffered from carsickness since childhood, but something about the combination of back-road jolting, swaying in the wind, and the peculiar smell of the van was bringing it all back with a vengeance.

'I didn't actually look at the weather forecast. It didn't seem important as we'd be inside all day.' He closed his eyes briefly, then immediately opened them when that made the sensation worse. Cold sweat prickled at his hairline, and he reached for the bottle of water tucked in his rucksack, taking careful sips.

'You ok?' Georgie glanced over.

'Fine,' he said.

She made a small disbelieving noise – not quite a sigh, not quite a word – and returned her attention to driving.

'I've got mints in the glove box if you're queasy. They always worked for me on the tournament transfer buses.'

'Na, I'm ok. I maybe just ate too much cheese.'

Georgie took the next bend at a cautious crawl, headlights cutting weakly through the gloom and rain.

'What the hell?' Kerr gaped ahead, and Georgie hit the brakes. The narrow road disappeared beneath a chocolate-brown lake of floodwater, bordered by a collapsed embankment where the hillside had given up its fight against gravity. A tree, roots exposed like obscene fingers, leaned drunkenly across half the gap, branches dipping into the muddy water.

'Holy shit.' Kerr leaned forward.

Georgie killed the engine. 'I'm not going to try to get through that.'

'I'll check how deep it is. Might be passable.'

'Kerr, I don't think—'

But he was already reaching for the door handle, a sudden need to do something, anything, propelling him out into the storm. The rain hit him like a physical blow, instantly soaking through his jacket. Wind snatched at his breath, cold fingers of air finding every gap in his clothing.

He approached the flood's edge, boots sinking slightly into the saturated grass verge. The water churned with unexpected violence, not the placid puddle it had appeared from a distance but a proper flow, carrying twigs and debris in its murky current. At the road's edge, he picked up a fallen branch and probed the water, finding no resistance until it was submerged too deep for the van.

This was a landslip and possibly one that hadn't finished. This road wasn't safe to be on.

He jogged back to the van. Water ran down his neck and into his boots. His jeans clung to his legs like a second skin. He yanked the door open and hopped into the passenger seat.

'Well?' Georgie asked.

'This isn't a safe place to be. I should probably call the police, but I doubt I'll have reception out here.' He checked his phone. 'Nope. The water's at least two feet deep and flowing fast. It's possibly still active.' He ran a hand through his sodden hair, flicking water droplets across the dashboard. 'Told you the A-road would've been better.'

The moment the words left his mouth, he regretted them. It wasn't Georgie's fault that the hillside had collapsed.

Georgie's lips pressed into a tight line.

'Sorry, that was uncalled for.'

'It's ok. I'll turn around and we'll go a different way.'

'Just be careful when you're turning. The verges are really soft.'

Kerr sat very still as she crunched the gears through a twenty-point turn and they took off in the other direction.

'Phew,' she said. 'That was a bit scary.'

'I'm not sure we're out of danger yet.'

'I meant the turn.'

'Oh... Yeah. Well done.'

She smirked. 'I've got a paper map in the pocket behind your seat. I see my phone has gone offline. Though it looks like there's a road up ahead.' She was looking at the offline version of the satnav on her phone screen.

Kerr fished around for the map and, using the torch on his phone, found where they were. 'I think that road takes us to a village called Strathbeck. It looks like it's only about four or five miles away. Maybe you should take it. We could see if there's somewhere we can get Wi-Fi and alert the police to that landslip. They'll want to close this road, I imagine.'

The road to Strathbeck twisted up a hill. Kerr gripped the door handle as the van tilted around another bend.

Kerr's clothes clung to him, his jeans chafing. The van's heater laboured heroically but hopelessly against this new wave of damp. His socks squished unpleasantly inside his boots. After going to the bother of buying those socks for the journey, he'd been distracted by cheese and forgotten to put the new ones on. Oh well. He could do that when they got to this village.

Wind buffeted the vehicle, pushing it towards the edge of the narrow road. Georgie corrected it with a tense movement, her knuckles white on the steering wheel. The wipers swiped frantically, struggling to keep pace with the deluge.

'Should be just around this bend,' Kerr said.

Strathbeck revealed itself with underwhelming modesty in the darkness – a scattering of buildings huddled around a crossroads with a few streetlamps illuminating more rain than anything else.

Georgie slowed the van to a crawl as they approached the centre. A pub with a weather-beaten sign and boarded-up windows stood on one corner. Its abandoned car park looked like a local dumping ground. Opposite was a row of cottages with identical pan-tile roofs and chimney pots. A small shop with metal shutters pulled down tight, and beside it, a tearoom with a 'Closed' sign hanging in the window.

'Ok, this place looks dead.' Kerr peered through the rain-streaked side window.

Georgie eased the van into the abandoned pub car park. She cut the engine, and instantly the rain seemed louder.

'I can piggyback on a signal here,' Kerr said. 'And send a message to the police about the road.' He flipped through his phone. Now was the time to put all his tech knowledge into action.

Georgie sat quietly while he figured it out.

A plastic bin tumbled across the road, propelled by a gust that rocked the van on its wheels.

'Well...' Georgie turned in her seat to face him. 'Do you think it would be safest just to stay here for a bit?'

The reality of their situation landed on Kerr like a wet blanket. They were stranded in a tiny village in the middle of nowhere, in a storm that showed no signs of abating, with little phone signal and limited options. But more unsettling than these practical concerns was the sudden, acute awareness of how small the van's cabin felt.

Without the distraction of driving, the space seemed to contract around them.

Kerr turned around and looked into the back of the van. 'I guess you've got everything we need.'

'I do. Would you like a hot drink?'

'Um... Ok.'

Georgie unbuckled herself and swivelled her seat around. She got up and started bustling around in the back.

'You don't have to go to any trouble—' he began.

'It's no trouble. I need a drink. This is just an inconvenient excuse.' She filled a small kettle from a water container.

There was something almost surreal about watching Georgie Porter – former tennis star, face on TV, subject of tabloid speculation – performing this mundane task. The gas hissed quietly as she lit the stove, the tiny blue flame a welcome spot of warmth.

She caught him watching and smiled wryly. 'Quite the career trajectory, eh? From Centre Court to camping snacks in a gale. My agent would have a fit if he could see me now.'

The quip caught Kerr off guard, and a reluctant laugh escaped before he could stop it.

'I don't know,' he said. 'There's probably a sponsorship opportunity in extreme weather picnicking.'

'You're not wrong.' Her smile widened. 'My agent suggested a travel blog. Think of the mileage I'd have got out of this.'

Rain continued to hammer on the roof, creating a strangely hypnotic white noise. Wind rocked the van occasionally, but inside, with the small stove glowing and the smell of tea filling the air, there was an unexpected cosiness that Kerr found himself appreciating.

She handed him a steaming mug and offered a packet of trail mix. His fingers brushed hers in the exchange, and an uncomfortable jolt struck Kerr. This was not good. Why couldn't he quit feeling like this?

If he could just ditch the pointless daydreams, and forget he'd fancied her forever and been gutted when she started dating Jake, then he could also put the brakes on the fantasies his mind was conjuring up for him.

He didn't need a relationship with someone who was likely to up and leave at any second. And Georgie Porter was a jetsetter. He didn't see her happily settling in one place when she was so used to travelling, and Kerr was happy in his teaching career. After having been burned by Anna, who'd upped and left him like that – not once, but twice, he didn't want to go through that again. Glenbriar was full of nice people. One day he'd meet a "normal" local girl, and that would be great. He didn't need to chase a shining star like Georgie. He could leave her sparkling out of his reach.

Jake was already furious with her for how things ended.

Getting him angry at me too?

Not part of the plan.

'This isn't quite how I meant to spend the evening,' Kerr said.

'Yeah... Sorry.' Georgie nibbled on the trail mix, with her gaze fixed on the dark windows.

Her eyes looked weary, and her shoulders tense. Perhaps she expected him to start berating her for refusing to take the motorway. But she was the driver. It was up to her which route to take. Landslips weren't that common, so it wasn't like she could have predicted this.

He wasn't usually grumpy, but being around Georgie made him tense – for so many reasons.

Now they just had to wait out the storm. But how long would that take? An hour? Two? All night. Kerr saw a certain serendipity, almost foresight, in buying those pyjamas, but he did *not* want to sleep in this van... or, more to the point, he did not want to sleep next to Georgie in this van.

If Jake ever found that out, it might end in fratricide.

Chapter Eleven

Georgie

The rain battered the van's roof like an impatient drummer with no sense of rhythm or restraint. Georgie sat cross-legged on the bench seat, both hands wrapped around her rapidly cooling mug of tea.

Outside, Strathbeck had disappeared beneath sheets of water, the village buildings reduced to smudged shadows beyond the glass. Inside, the heater hummed with mechanical determination, pushing out air that had progressed from 'slightly less cold than outside' to 'almost warm if you sat directly in front of it.'

Georgie tucked that persistent strand of hair behind her ear, a nervous habit she'd had since her playing days. She'd do it repeatedly as she waited to return serve. Kerr sat opposite her, shoulders rigid, eyes fixed on his phone, still trying to do something with it, though she wasn't sure exactly what. It wasn't like they could call someone and ask for the bad weather to be switched off.

'More tea?' she said.

Kerr glanced up briefly. 'No, thanks.' His attention returned to his phone.

Oh god, this was going to be a long evening. Centre Court nerves were nothing compared to this. At least in tennis, she'd known what was expected of her – the rules, the boundaries, the path to victory. This was all strange.

'Bet you're regretting getting into a vehicle with me now,' she said.

'It is what it is.' With a sigh, he peered out of the window. What did he expect to see? 'The landslip road is shut now, so my message must have got through. I'm getting on and off Wi-Fi. The traffic update said road closures.'

Georgie took a sip of her green tea. 'That's good.'

'I remember reading about a landslip around here ages ago. Never occurred to me that I might get stuck in one. I think there was one near Glenbriar about twenty years ago. I was only eight. Mum's friend lived in a house that nearly got washed away.'

'I remember that. It was really close to the main road.'

'Yeah, and the hill was filled in after with rocks and covered with that big mesh stuff.'

She nodded. 'I guess grass has grown over it now because I can't even remember exactly where that was.'

Discussing twenty-year-old landslips in Glenbriar seemed like a safe enough subject, but Georgie's thoughts circled around those days. She hadn't known Kerr that early on. Her family had lived in the village of Dairvin around the loch from Glenbriar, and she'd gone to the tiny little primary school. It wasn't until high school that she'd met Kerr... through Jake. Whenever conversations went back to the past, the danger of finding Jake lingered.

A particularly violent gust rocked them slightly, the motion sending a splash of tea over the rim of her mug and onto her fingers. She set the mug down hastily, wiping her hand on a dishcloth.

'What possessed you to do this?' Kerr asked.

'I'm not confident on motorways. I told you.'

'I don't mean that. I mean, why did you get a campervan? Do you really enjoy touring about in this? Wouldn't you prefer to be in a five-star hotel?'

'Maybe.' She shrugged and looked away. 'But the tour wasn't always that glam. Sometimes the hotels were terrible. And there was no freedom. I guess this is me rebelling and doing something wild. I don't plan to live like this forever. The whole washing clothes in a campsite utility room and emptying chemical waste tanks isn't really my scene. But there's something nice about being able to roam.'

His eyes scanned around the van. 'I can see the appeal. I always wanted to hire something like this during the school holidays, but I never got around to it yet. The summer this year was spent looking for a house. I only just moved into the one on Kirk Lane. It's a bit small to be honest, but there's not a lot of choice in the town.'

'Were you back living with your parents before?'

'No. They would have had me, but I was staying with Eddie and his partner. It felt a bit more like my own space. My mum is a sweetheart, but she fusses.'

'It's funny that Eddie is your friend when he used to be our teacher.'

Kerr smiled. 'I know. We joke about how grossed out people would be if I came back and we became lovers, not friends. The age gap would have got all the tongues wagging.'

Georgie let out a laugh. 'Yeah, that would have fed the gossips forever. But... Well, I know Eddie's gay, but you're not, are you?'

He shook his head. 'No, but it's a laugh thinking about it. And he's such a great mate, better than anyone of my own age. He's twenty-five years older than me, but it doesn't feel like that.'

'It's funny how that can happen. I had a coach like that once. He was much older than me, but we got on so well. It really is just a number. Especially as we get older.' She caught his eye and, for a moment, they just looked at each other. It wasn't awkward, but many unspoken thoughts passed between them, and Georgie's heart fluttered. Something like this had happened at Jake's graduation party. It had only been a moment, but it had hit her hard and unsettled her.

She and Jake had never slept together, and Jake had wanted that to be their first time together, but he'd got too drunk. And after Georgie had had the encounter with Kerr, she left. Nothing had happened, but something inside her felt off.

He held her gaze like he wasn't in a rush to look away, and her pulse jumped. That strange sensation was building in her again, only this time she didn't want to run. Staring into his soft hazel eyes made her feel she was somewhere safe and warm. The faint scruff on his jaw gave him a rugged edge, and he had the kind of build that didn't need showing off but was there for anyone to see – broad shoulders, thick forearms and long fingers with very clean nails. But it wasn't just his looks. He gave her a gentle smile, and he felt like a solid and reliable person to be with. If she had to be stranded with someone, she wouldn't have necessarily chosen him for obvious reasons, but it could have been a lot worse.

Stability was something she never felt around Jake. He was the opposite – unpredictable and moody.

'I'm really sorry about this.' She blinked, breaking the connection.

Kerr was still watching her. 'You don't control the weather.'

'I shouldn't have insisted on the back roads. And I offered to drive here in the first place. And I... well, I feel like an idiot.'

'Don't. It's ok.' His smile grew a little wider.

'Really?'

'Yeah. It's an adventure, right?'

'Right.' Their gazes linked again.

The wind threw another handful of rain against the windows, the sound like gravel hitting glass. The words she felt she needed to say were too large for her throat.

'I think…' She faltered, then pushed forward. 'I'm really sorry about what happened. With Jake.'

Kerr's shoulders tensed, and he looked away. 'You mean when he found out on TV that you were dating a top-ten player?'

'Yeah. But it's not what you think. I was struggling. My form was slipping, and it was the start of my shoulder giving me hell. My ranking was in freefall.'

'I remember,' Kerr said. 'But it's hardly an excuse.'

'I know. But my manager at the time had been pushing an idea for months. A "strategic relationship" with Stefan Varis.' She almost laughed at how ridiculous it sounded now, but the fact she and Jake were never together made everyone on her team question the relationship. Her manager decided the time to dump Jake was right… and maybe that was the truth. But it shouldn't have been up to him. 'Stefan was ranked sixth in the world, a sponsor darling, the whole package. My manager said it would keep me relevant, get the publicity machine going again while I was struggling with my game. The tabloids would eat it up.'

Kerr's expression remained neutral, but his eyes never left her face.

'I said no at first. Jake and I had been together for a while at that point… But you know, we never…'

'Never what?'

'Nothing… But anyway, my primary sponsor started making noise about not renewing. I had a really bad start to the clay court season, and my manager kept saying how a high-profile relationship would keep me "in the conversation", but my current relationship with Jake just looked like a smokescreen.' And it was. She liked the security of being able to tell the press, fans, and other players that she had a boyfriend, even if she rarely saw him, and they communicated mostly by text.

The rain drummed a steady accompaniment to her confession on the van roof.

'I convinced myself it would just be for a few months. Some public appearances, holding hands at a few events, nothing serious.' She shook her head at her own naivety... and the lie. 'But it wasn't quite how it happened. And my manager... well, he managed it all, or he said he did.'

So much for "feel the fear and do it anyway". She'd been such a coward with Jake. And the pain she'd caused him might be irrevocable. She might have been better not even trying.

'The next week, we had photos of Stefan and me "looking cosy" at a charity event my manager had arranged. I had no idea he hadn't told Jake. He said he would. Then it all happened so fast. Jake sent me messages. Even your mum sent me one. It wasn't nasty. In fact, it was really kind, but I felt like I'd disappointed her so much.' Georgie closed her eyes briefly. 'And to be honest, Stefan was a nice guy. He understood me.'

Kerr's jaw tightened, but he remained silent.

'Though it wasn't love or anything like that.'

Outside, a car's headlights briefly cut through the gloom as it passed the car park, the light sliding across their faces like a searchlight before disappearing again.

'I hate the way Jake found out. It hurt him so much, and I've regretted it every day since.'

She looked up, meeting Kerr's gaze. 'I'm not asking for forgiveness. I just wanted to see Jake and tell him. Apologise for how things were. It would have been best for both of us if I'd split up with him when I left Glenbriar. The long-distance thing didn't work, and then...' She swallowed.

'You didn't have the nerve to break up with him?' Kerr folded his arms.

'Yes. I didn't have the guts to tell him I didn't want to keep seeing him. I knew how hurt he'd be.'

'Why did you go out with him in the first place?'

Georgie huffed out a laugh. 'Because he asked me.' And she felt a bit sorry for him. Not exactly the best reason to start a relationship, but she'd only been eighteen and hadn't worked that out.

'I get that being caught between your career and your relationship, with all the pressure to perform and stay relevant, must have been tricky,' Kerr said. 'But it's not really my place to forgive you. That's Jake's call.'

'Yep,' she said quietly.

'And really.' Kerr raised his eyebrows. 'Isn't it better to leave it in the past?'

She lowered her eyes and nodded. 'Maybe.' She briefly glanced up at him. 'It would probably be best if I just went back to London and let sleeping dogs lie, wouldn't it?'

He tapped his finger on the table. 'As far as Jake's concerned, probably. But if you're really interested in the MUGA and doing something in Glenbriar, then that's your call.'

Georgie got up with a sigh and pulled the van's curtains closed, sealing them off from the world. Kerr turned around and did the ones behind him.

'I'm really not sure what I want to do. I think that's part of my problem.'

'Sometimes it takes a while to figure it out. I was lucky to meet Eddie when I was in a bad place. He's like a wise owl.'

She smiled at the vision. The only light came from a small reading lamp mounted above the bench seat. The storm continued its assault, but the sound had shifted from immediate threat to an ambient backdrop.

'Are you hungry?' she asked. 'I've got some pasta, or I could make sandwiches.'

'Um, ok, a sandwich would be good.' Kerr rolled his shoulders. 'Don't go to any trouble though.'

She busied herself with retrieving food from the cabinet and the little fridge. Whether she'd cleared the air or just caused even more problems remained to be seen. Her chest felt lighter having shared some of it, but tension still gripped her neck and upper arms. Perhaps closure with Jake wasn't what she really needed, but something completely new. Could she really find that in Glenbriar?

Chapter Twelve

Kerr

Georgie's story about Jake had been telling.

Kerr bit into the sandwich – cheese and some kind of tangy pickle – and chewed slowly.

She clearly regretted how they'd broken up. It seemed to go against her 'feel the fear and do it anyway' motto. But honestly the best place for her regrets was somewhere alone, far from Jake. Opening things up with him again wasn't a good plan. If she wanted to stay in Glenbriar, then that was her call, and it wouldn't cause too many issues... as long as Jake stayed in London, and Kerr kept out of her way. Self-preservation.

But he sensed her uncertainty. Maybe Glenbriar wasn't her kind of place. She was used to more exciting places.

He watched her from across the small table as she faffed with the kettle and frowned. A few months ago he wouldn't have thought Georgie cooking in a campervan was likely either, and yet it was happening, so maybe he'd misjudged her.

She smiled at him, and his insides leapt. They were stuck in a very small space together, and it was scrambling his brain good and proper. Thoughts he'd suppressed for years were pushing their way to the front of his mind, making the 'what ifs' so strong he half suspected Georgie might hear them.

What if she'd dated him and not Jake? He'd been too young when they'd first got together, but he'd liked her, and Jake knew it. But that was Jake, in a nutshell. He often pulled stunts like that, thinking he was smart. But if things went wrong, he dipped so hard everyone suffered. With Jake in London, it was easier to detach, but Kerr didn't want to fall out permanently with his brother. His family was important to him.

He returned the smile, not sure what else to do.

A particularly violent gust rocked the van.

Something clattered against the side – a loud, scraping bang – followed by another thud that made the whole structure shudder.

Kerr got up fast, the remains of his sandwich forgotten. Georgie's eyes were wide as she turned to the curtained window behind her.

'What the hell was that?' She split the curtains and looked out.

'No idea.' Kerr moved to another window and pulled back the curtain. Nothing but darkness and sheets of rain sliding down the glass in silver streaks. He squinted but couldn't make out anything.

Another rattle followed, lower down this time.

Georgie moved closer to where he was standing and peered out the same window, her arm brushing his as she pushed the curtain wider. 'What do you think it was?'

'This car park is full of junk. Something probably blew away.'

'What if it's damaged the side panel? Or knocked something loose?'

'I'm not sure how we would know that without going outside.'

She shook her head. 'Yeah... I just hope water can't get in somewhere.'

Kerr looked back out, the wind hurling rain at the glass with relentless force. 'We could have a look, but we'll get soaked.'

Another gust hit, less aggressive this time. Georgie stepped back, arms folded tight across her chest. 'I'll go and look. You stay inside.'

She reached for her jacket and tugged it on. Before Kerr could argue further, she was at the door.

'I'll come with you.' He wasn't going to sit here like a useless idiot.

'You don't have to. I'm the one who dragged you here, after all.' She pulled a large torch from a storage compartment.

'We're in it together.' Kerr grabbed his waterproof jacket from where it had barely dried since their earlier drenching. His mind did a weird, fleeting jump from the damp jacket to the warm socks and pyjamas he had in the carrier bag from the supermarket. Maybe he should just put them on, abandon the idea of getting home tonight, and sleep in the van... Only one problem... Only one bed.

Outside was chaos – rain driving horizontally, wind whipping around the van with malicious glee. They staggered around to the back, looking for the source of the noise.

A spray of grit hit Kerr in the face as they rounded the corner of the van, the torch beam bobbing ahead of them like a ship's lantern in a storm. Georgie's hood flapped violently in the wind, her hair already soaked and sticking to her cheeks.

'There – look!' she shouted over the wind.

The torch caught on something large and angular, half wedged under the back wheel arch. Kerr squinted against the rain. A rusted metal shelf, by the look of it – one of those freestanding units you might find in a shed, now twisted and broken.

'Must've come off that heap of crap.' Georgie jabbed the light towards a sagging pile of pallets, tarpaulins and unidentifiable shapes.

Kerr crouched to yank the shelf free, the cold biting through the knees of his jeans. It clanged against the side panel as it came loose, another screech of metal on metal.

'Shit. Check I haven't damaged something,' he muttered, dragging it clear and tossing it into a puddle.

Georgie moved in beside him, running her hand along the van's side. 'It might be a bit scuffed, but it's not cracked.'

Kerr lifted the rusty shelf and dragged it away from the van, then placed it down beside a stone wall.

Georgie held the torch high as he rammed some cracked bricks on top of it. Hopefully that would stop it moving again.

'Bloody rain,' she said. 'Feels like needles.'

'The tyres seem ok.' Kerr straightened up, water trickling down the back of his neck. 'Is anything else damaged?'

'Doesn't look like it.' She ran her fingers along the side panel. 'Should we move the van somewhere else? Is this safe?'

'I honestly don't think we'll find anywhere better. This wind could blow anything from anywhere.'

'True.' She pulled a face. 'Should we stay here... as in overnight? Or do you want to try to get home?'

'Let's get back inside before we decide anything.'

They made their way back to the door, slipping slightly in the mud

'God, this is grim,' Georgie muttered.

'You think?'

She let out a breath that was almost a laugh, and Kerr's insides squirmed. He was such a fool. Whenever he saw Georgie – even on TV – he regressed to being a lovesick teenager. And being stuck in close proximity like this wasn't helping one bit.

'Let's get back in before my fingers drop off.' She pulled open the door, and Kerr followed, his trainers squelching.

'At least the van has character now,' Kerr said. 'Unlike those soulless hotel rooms.'

Georgie prised off her jacket and hung it over the driver's seat. 'Character being some scuffs on the paintwork?'

'Exactly.'

Kerr's damp clothing clung to him, and each movement sent a fresh wave of discomfort through his limbs. Across the narrow space, Georgie wasn't faring any better – her shoulders trembled visibly as she pulled off her wet shoes. He sat in the passenger seat and did the same.

'Thank god I bought those dry socks.'

'You tempted fate,' she said.

'Something like that.'

'Well...' She twisted her lips into a side pout. 'Do you want to stay here tonight? I can pull the bed out. And you've even got pyjamas.'

He raised an eyebrow at her. 'That might turn out to be my best impulse buy ever.'

'Exactly... And I've got enough spare cushions that we could make a pillow wall, so we don't have to be too close or worry about...' She gave a little shrug '...anything.'

Anything? As in the risk of him acting on years of unspoken feelings... that hopefully she knew nothing about.

'Ok.' He nodded. 'Right now, I just want to get warm.'

'I'll boil the kettle, and I have hot-water bottles.'

An awkward silence descended as they looked at each other. The van, while cleverly designed, offered precisely zero privacy. No separate changing room, no convenient screen, not even a shower curtain to duck behind. The built-in bathroom was too small to change in. She was probably used to getting changed in front of people, and Kerr wouldn't have been that bothered normally either. But with her...

'I'll turn around.' Georgie gathered some dry clothes from the cupboard. 'I won't look.'

'Look if you want. I have nothing to hide.'

She raised an eyebrow. 'I'm so cold I really don't care.' She pulled her sweater over her head and cast it aside. Kerr swallowed as she stood before him in a strawberry pink bra working on the fastening of her trousers.

Fuck it. Help. He turned away, looking for the bag with the warm socks and pyjamas in it.

He fixed his gaze firmly on the rain-streaked windscreen as he took off his top. Despite his best intentions, he was acutely aware of every sound behind him – the soft rustle of fabric, the gentle thud of wet clothes hitting the floor.

Swallowing hard, he took off his soaked jeans and boxer briefs together and pulled on the new pyjamas as fast as he could.

He turned to find her dressed in a low-cut vest top and a pair of sleep shorts that revealed her long, athletically toned legs. It wasn't much different from some of her tennis outfits, except for her obvious lack of underwear.

Again, not good. Or possibly too good. Depending on which result he wanted to induce.

She tugged the band from her ponytail and let her hair fall loose.

'I'll give this a quick dry.' She pulled out a little dryer and plugged it in.

'Is this bathroom safe to use?' Kerr peered inside it.

'Yes, though my shoulders aren't as big as yours. You might get wedged in.'

He raised an eyebrow. 'Nice.'

Just as well he didn't have to sit to pee. This had to be the smallest bathroom he'd ever been in. The hairdryer was buzzing when he came out, and Georgie looked like a picture-perfect campervan girl getting ready for a cosy night in. Who would ever have known they'd just weathered a storm and were stuck in the middle of nowhere between landslips and floods?

'There we are.' She tucked the dryer away and lifted a couple of hot water bottles, her chestnut hair now tumbling over her shoulders, softening her look. Wow, she was really beautiful. 'How about you fill them up while I pull out the bed?'

Kerr took them and poured the water inside them, half watching as she shifted about at the back, until the two bench seats had joined in the middle. She crawled over them, setting out pillows.

Really, could she not do that? Seeing her crouched on the bed like that in that skimpy outfit made all his blood rush south.

She placed some cushions down the middle, then pulled a duvet from an overhead locker. 'We'll have to share this. So no hogging.'

Kerr snorted, handed her a hot water bottle and sat on one side of the pillow wall.

'I'll just use the loo.' Georgie crossed the van, and Kerr used her absence to crawl into the bed. Stretching this duvet over them both with the pillows down the middle would be interesting. It wasn't particularly big.

Georgie returned and got into the other side of the bed. She tugged the duvet over herself, pulling it off Kerr.

'Hey.'

'Ah...' she sat up. 'This isn't exactly going to work, is it?'

'Maybe we should move the pillows and risk it. All we're planning on is sleeping, right?'

'Right.' She lifted a pillow and pushed one at the edge beside her. Then she lifted the other one, and Kerr thought for a moment she was planning on leaning over him and tucking it down the side of him. Before she could do it, he took it from her and did it himself. It was better there as it provided a shield against the side of the van, but it left him just a hair's breadth from her.

He lay stiffly beside her. The van creaked and shifted with each gust of wind, while inside, the atmosphere was charged with a different kind of tension.

This was dangerously close to things he'd dreamed of since his school days. Memories assaulted his brain. How furious he'd been when Jake announced he was dating Georgie. How he'd had to hide those feelings. His parents had brought him up to respect his big brother, and he did, though he wasn't convinced that respect always went both ways. Deep down, he'd never forgiven Jake for dating Georgie. Not really. How could he? Because Jake knew. He pretended not to, or that he'd forgotten about Kerr liking Georgie. But he hadn't. And Kerr couldn't shake the sense that Jake had done it to annoy him or taunt him. It came not long after Kerr had been accepted onto the school junior tennis team – when Jake hadn't been picked. It felt more like revenge than a coincidence.

A particularly violent shiver ran through Georgie.

'Sorry,' she whispered. 'I think it's just the sound that's making me cold.'

A slight shudder ran through Kerr too. 'Maybe.'

'Or maybe my instincts are to use body heat to warm up and they're rebelling because I'm keeping them away from the heat.'

Kerr snorted. How could he help it? 'Is that your way of saying you want to cuddle up? Because surely you don't. Not with your ex's little brother.'

'My brain knows I shouldn't want to, but my body is cold and does want to.'

He nodded at the dark ceiling. 'Ok,' he said gruffly.

'Are you serious?'

'Well, you said it first. And only to keep warm. I'm not suggesting that we jump each other. It's literally to stop us from freezing to death.'

Georgie hesitated, then shifted closer so her back was against him, her body fitting against his side so perfectly. Kerr inhaled sharply, turning slightly and draping his arm over her, making himself the big spoon. And, hell, did it feel good?

'That's better,' she said.

Kerr made a non-committal sound in response, not trusting himself to speak. The scent of her filled his senses, the warmth of her body seeping through the thin pyjama top.

This was a thing of beauty. Nothing else need happen ever. Because he'd stolen something he'd wanted for so long. Closing his eyes, he relaxed, holding her close.

Outside, the wind still howled its discontent, rain lashing against the metal shell of their sanctuary. Inside, two people with a tangled past breathed in sync. Kerr breathed in her hair and let his mind drift.

For this moment, she was his. If he could press the pause button on life, he would. He could just live here and forget everything else. Forget who he was, where he was, what he was doing here, and most of all that the woman in his arms was someone he could never have.

Not unless he wanted to hurt his brother even more. And was it worth it for someone who might take off at the first opportunity? Just like Anna had done. And he didn't want to put himself through that again.

Chapter Thirteen

Georgie

Georgie woke with a start, momentarily disorientated. The bed in the campervan was the same, but the solid warmth against her back was different. Her sleep-fogged brain took several seconds to work out that it was Kerr. He breathed deeply and evenly, and Georgie closed her eyes. Was it wrong to be enjoying this so much?

She and Jake had never got this far. And that was partly down to her. If she'd really wanted it, she could have made it happen.

Her eyes stayed shut. This way, she could avoid facing harsh reality, and maybe this moment would last longer... as long as possible.

Kerr and Jake may look alike, but Kerr was much more easy-going. Even when he was grumpy, he didn't have the same edge. Back at school, she remembered Kerr as smiley and a bit of a joker. She'd seen some of that when they'd played tennis and when she'd watched him interact with Eddie. Of course he was more guarded with her – their history dictated it.

'Morning.' Kerr's deep voice vibrated against her neck, and she twitched involuntarily.

'Hey.' She didn't look around, move, or do anything that might draw attention to the fact he was still spooning her and had been all night. She wanted to hold on to this feeling. Being tall, she liked being with men who were taller, giving her that feeling of being cocooned and comforted. 'It sounds like the storm's died down a bit.'

'Yeah, it does.' He lifted his arm and rolled away with a slight groan.

Georgie's insides crumpled at the loss of contact. She wanted to curl into a ball and hide. Facing anything alone seemed too big an ask.

What the hell?

Since when had she been such a quitter?

NEVER!

She was a fighter, and she had to keep going – feel the fear and do it anyway. Though she wasn't entirely sure what she was afraid of exactly. Perhaps the giant can of worms she would open if she got too close to Kerr – either physically or emotionally?

'We should get going.' She forced herself to sit up.

Kerr glanced at her, running a hand through his dishevelled hair. 'I guess.'

'I've got stuff we can eat for breakfast. And now that it's daylight, we'll be able to see better. Hopefully, we won't run into any more landslips.'

'Yeah. Let's hope.'

'There should be enough water for a shower, if you want one,' Georgie said.

'Why? Do I smell?' Kerr pulled out his T-shirt and sniffed.

He did... but not badly. In fact, whatever cologne he wore was enough to drive her over the edge. It was crisp and citrusy at first, like grapefruit or lemon, but through the night it had got more sensual and smoky with undertones of something else, possibly sandalwood. Whatever it was, she would quite happily inhale it all day long.

'No. I just thought you might want to try my first-class facilities.'

He raised an eyebrow, then grinned. 'Um... Ok. Though you realise I barely fit in that bathroom.'

'Don't exaggerate.' She smirked at him, but he was probably right. He must be about six foot three, and his shoulders were very broad. Maybe her wayward mind was only pushing him to do this, so she could get a view of him topless if he decided to come out wrapped only in a towel.

Seriously? She was the one who needed a cold shower. Or maybe she should just bash her unhinged head off a wall. She'd turned into a maniac.

'Ok. I'll give it a go.'

She went to the loo, brushed her teeth, then found him a towel. They did a bit of a dance to avoid each other in the small space. Once he was in, she folded away the duvet and pushed the bed back to the two benches. She opened the curtains a crack and saw a rather grey and wet scene. At least the wind had stopped, though it was still raining.

Her little kitchen area had a good stock of healthy breakfasts. Hopefully Kerr would be OK with Greek yoghurt, berries, and granola. There was also peanut butter, protein bars, and some chia pots she'd prepped in little jars. Once a tennis player and all that. The bathroom door clicked open. She didn't look up straightaway. No need to act like a hormonal teenager, though she was worse even than that right now.

The scent hit her before anything else. Warm skin and steam, edged with her own midnight bloom shower gel. It suited him. How was it even possible that it smelled different on him? But it did, and hell, did it send sparks to every nerve end? Her hand faltered over the bag of granola.

'You didn't get stuck then?' she asked, not directly looking at him, but he was visible in her peripheral vision.

'Just about.' Kerr's voice was rougher than before, the kind of rough that curled low in her belly.

She risked a glance and nearly dropped the bag.

Sweet mother of—

He was standing by the wardrobe area in nothing but a very small towel. Low on the hips. Damp hair shoved back. Water still glistened on his shoulders. Broad. Solid. All long limbs and lean muscle. Christ. He was hotter than she'd ever imagined.

'I hope you aren't expecting a robe and slippers,' she said, instantly feeling like a twat, but words were better than gaping.

'Of course I was.' He tugged the towel a little tighter, though not much. 'So much for those first-class facilities.' He lifted the jeans he'd hung up to dry last night.

'Ah, yes. I'm slipping.'

'These feel dry, at least.' He lifted his boxer briefs and dropped the towel. Just like that. No hesitation.

Georgie clamped her eyes forward. *Do not look.* There was breakfast. Important breakfast. Life-saving breakfast.

Except... the van had windows that acted like mirrors. Bloody helpful mirrors.

She caught a flash of him in the reflection as he pulled on his boxers, then his jeans. She swallowed hard.

'The heater must have done something,' he said. 'This stuff is dry, but my jeans could do with some fabric softener.'

She turned with what she hoped was a neutral expression. 'Oh... That's a shame.'

He glanced at her, one eyebrow raised, then pulled on his shirt with a slight smirk. Did he know what a hot bastard he was?

'What are you making?' He stepped closer.

'I, um, have a selection.' She suddenly remembered she was still in her jammies. Braless. And dammit did her treacherous nips give her away, pushing their way through the soft fabric like they were determined to get to Kerr. 'You can choose whatever you like. I'm going for my shower.'

'I hope I didn't use all the hot water,' he said.

'No worries.' She really didn't care. Icy water might shock some sense into her and really she'd do anything to get away from him. He was doing all kinds of things to her, and she liked it. Far. Too. Much.

This was not sensible.

The shower was more lukewarm than hot, but she didn't hang around. A quick rinse, a swipe of shower gel, and a blast of cold right at the end just to hammer the message home. No lingering thoughts about Kerr. No getting carried away. No fantasising about him in only a towel. Or out of one.

She towelled off and stepped back into the steamy van in her towel. He was sitting at the bench now, nursing a mug of tea with a bowl of muesli in front of him.

Good.

She grabbed clean knickers, leggings, a sports bra and hoodie from her storage cubby and dropped her towel, just like he'd done.

She glanced sideways.

Kerr was still staring at the window, foot tapping slowly. Not watching. Not obviously, anyway.

She changed quickly. Years of locker rooms had taught her speed and efficiency, but this wasn't the same. This wasn't a bunch of sweaty women, half-listening to match reports and stuffing protein bars in their faces. This was Kerr. And he was ten feet away. And the air between them was thicker than the steam still lingering in the tiny bathroom.

When she turned back, he gave her a brief glance, then looked down at his tea. If he'd seen anything, he gave no indication.

'You ok?' she asked. 'Is the breakfast up to scratch?'

'Yeah. It's good.'

She plated up her yoghurt and berries and sat opposite him.

They ate in relative silence. Not awkward exactly, but definitely something. Words felt like too much and not enough at the same time. She wasn't sure if she should break it or let it stretch between them like a rubber band, waiting to snap.

He caught her eye, and a stupid jolt of heat zipped through her.

'Let's see what it looks like outside.' He pulled back the curtain.

'Grim. I already looked.' Georgie finished off her breakfast, and they cleared up together, not speaking. Then Georgie moved to the driver's seat while he strapped in beside her. The windscreen was still streaked with rain, but the world outside was at least visible now.

She started the engine as he clicked his seatbelt into place.

'Ready?' she asked.

'As I'll ever be.'

She headed back towards the road they'd turned off the night before.

'I think it would be a really good idea to take the main road home,' Kerr said after a while. 'I know you prefer back roads.'

'They're safer.' Georgie gripped the wheel.

'But the main roads have less chance of landslips or sudden road closures.'

'That one near Glenbriar was on a main road.'

He gave her a sideways look. 'Seriously? I'm just saying... the main road's probably clear. And I can help you. We'll do it together.'

She didn't answer right away, letting the word settle. *Together.*

'How? Are you going to grab the wheel or something?'

'No. But how about you treat it like a driving lesson? Think of it as building confidence.'

'Oh my God.' She turned fully towards him for a second, one brow raised. 'You just want an excuse to mansplain.'

'I'm a teacher. It goes with the territory.'

She snorted. 'Oh great.'

He shrugged, still half-smirking. 'Come on. Where's that Georgie Porter spirit? You can do this.'

She gave him a look. 'Ok.' With a long, slow inhale, she nodded. 'Find the way to the motorway and we'll do it.'

The wipers squeaked across the windscreen, clearing thin sheets of drizzle as Georgie followed the twisty roads towards the motorway. It wasn't just around the corner, so she had time to think. To worry – or chicken out. But she wouldn't. Her determined streak was back.

Feel the fear and do it anyway.

They reached a junction where a sign pointed to the M8, busy even on a Sunday morning. Georgie's hands tightened on the wheel.

'Are you ok?' Kerr said quietly.

Georgie stared at the sign. 'I'm fine.' She'd made up her mind, and she was doing it. She flipped the indicator, signalling her intention. Kerr shifted slightly in his seat, not obviously watching her but somehow radiating a steady presence that felt reassuring.

The van climbed the gentle incline of the on-ramp, the main road coming into view ahead – two lanes in each direction, vehicles moving at a steady clip despite the persistent drizzle. Her palms began to sweat, her breath coming shorter as she checked her mirrors with almost frantic frequency. But it was no worse than playing the top seed on Centre Court.

She kept her eyes on the road, maintaining a steady speed as a lorry passed them in the outside lane. The habitual panic fluttered at the edges of her consciousness, but it remained manageable.

Kerr smiled. She felt it rather than saw it as she didn't dare take her eyes off the road. 'My mum made me drive this road two days after I passed my test,' he said. 'I was petrified. But I'm glad she did. Once you get over that initial fear, you'll never look back.'

'I hope so.'

Motorways definitely weren't as scenic as the back roads, but they got back to Glenbriar a lot quicker – and even there, the change of season was obvious, with banks of trees turning bronze and gold and the verges scattered with fallen leaves. Kerr had chatted in his easy way, but Georgie felt like they hadn't really *said* much. Nothing earth shattering anyway. Which was probably just as well. They'd skirted around mentioning how they slept last night, or how they'd dressed that morning.

'You can drop me at the end of Kirk Lane,' Kerr said, as they passed the Stagger Inn on the main street. A sign in the window advertised the upcoming Autumn Gold Festival.

Georgie nodded and pulled into the edge close to the turnoff that led to Kirk Lane. 'Is this ok?'

Kerr smiled. 'Yeah, this is great.'

'That was a rather eventful day, wasn't it?'

'You're not wrong. I've almost forgotten what we were actually meant to be doing. We still have to report on the MUGA meeting to Amanda.'

'I'll message her and arrange a date.'

'No doubt.'

A beat of silence stretched between them before Kerr reached for his rucksack.

'Thanks for pushing me to try the motorway,' she said. 'I don't think I would ever have done it without that nudge.'

'No worries. And at the risk of sounding patronising, you handled it really well.'

She grinned. 'Thanks, Mr Mansplainer.'

He returned her smile and gave her a little wave. 'Any time.'

'Bye.' Georgie watched him walk away, his figure growing smaller as he headed up the hill. She couldn't decide if she felt disappointed or relieved that she was back on her own.

She put the van in gear and pulled away, ready to return to Heather Glen, though her chest felt oddly bereft. The purpose she'd enjoyed all day yesterday had quickly ebbed, and she was adrift in the sea of uncertainty again.

The fact that Georgie's three oldest school friends had jobs that meant they were available during the week was really helpful. Not only because it meant Georgie didn't have to wait until the weekend to see them, but because it made her feel less of a loose end. Maybe that was silly. After all, Hayley, Elise and Genevieve all had jobs, while Georgie technically didn't, but the thought of meeting up with them again gave her something to look forward to. And a good reason to stop thinking about Kerr for five minutes.

Georgie made her way into Glenbriar on Tuesday afternoon to the Cosy Bean Café. When she'd lived here before, the café had been tucked into a narrow shopfront on the high street, but it had since relocated to a purpose-built timber cabin nestled among silver birch trees near the edge of Loch Briar. Their pale trunks shimmered against a backdrop of amber and russet foliage, the forest floor scattered with crisp leaves that crunched underfoot. This was where the town met the loch, and the winding path along the shoreline was busy with dog walkers and bundled-up couples enjoying the crisp air. No doubt that was why the owner had moved – the steady flow of passing trade was hard to resist.

When Hayley had done Georgie's hair the previous week, she'd suggested getting together for a coffee and reuniting the old school friends. While the idea gave Georgie the warm fuzzies, she also had some nervous flutters.

Inside, the café was warm and inviting, with wooden beams strung with fairy lights and tiny pumpkins dotting the windowsills. A chalkboard sign by the counter advertised the season's specials: cinnamon swirls, butternut squash soup, and spiced apple traybake. Georgie fancied a pumpkin spiced latte – why not? Autumn was in full swing, and here, it seemed to touch everything.

Georgie spotted her friends before they saw her. Was she late? Or had they come early to gossip before she arrived? They clustered around a corner table, their heads bent close in animated conversation.

As with everything else in her old life, Georgie hadn't kept in touch with these girls. Did they really want her back in their lives? Or was Hayley just being polite? Maybe they didn't expect her to stick around, and this was just lip service. Well, she'd take it, because she *wasn't* planning on staying long term, was she? Passing friends were better than no friends.

Hayley's dark waves tumbled over her shoulders as she laughed at something Elise had said, while Genevieve cradled a baby bump with one hand, the other wrapped around a steaming mug. Georgie knew she was pregnant. Hayley had got her up to speed with all the gossip during her hair appointment but seeing her like that hit hard. Babies and children had always seemed like something other people did. It wasn't impossible to be a mother on tour. Some players did it, but Georgie's managers and coaches had made it clear she shouldn't even think about it – even if they hadn't said it outright.

How easily led was I?

The more she thought about it, the more she realised she'd let people rule her life for too long. But it had been so easy. Now she was out in the big-bad world making decisions for herself, she didn't have a clue what to do next.

'Georgie!' Hayley's face lit up as she spotted her. 'Get over here, you absolute stranger!'

The hugs were warm and genuine, if slightly awkward with all the years that had passed. Elise, sleek and sophisticated in tailored trousers and a silk blouse, held her a second longer than necessary. They'd reconnected briefly at the tennis open day, but opportunities to talk had been slim that day.

'This must be hard,' Elise murmured, pulling back to study Georgie's face. 'I know how you feel. The three of us had a bit of a split, but we're all good now. I just made some mistakes.'

'Oh?' Georgie took a seat. 'I guess I'm guilty of lots of them.'

'Not at all.' Genevieve draped her sage green wrap over her rounded belly. 'You had a pretty full-on career.'

Georgie smiled. 'I'm sure you all did too. I was just sucked into a completely different world, and it was hard to think about life back here.'

'I bet.' Hayley patted her arm. The conversation flowed, and Georgie listened to all the goings on she'd missed, including the hilarious story of how Genevieve had got engaged to Hayley's brother Finlay, and how Hayley in turn had fallen for her brother's best friend. Then Elise pitched in with the mindboggling tale of how she'd been engaged to both Hayley's brother and cousin, become notorious in the town for breaking off both engagements, and was now dating one of her ex's best friends. Honestly, they couldn't have made it up.

A waitress approached and took Georgie's order with poorly concealed awe, her eyes darting repeatedly to Georgie's face as if confirming she really was *that* tennis player.

'It's funny being out with someone more famous than Genevieve,' Hayley observed with a smirk once the girl had left.

'I'm not famous,' Genevieve said.

'You kind of are.'

Georgie had to wait until they explained that Genevieve had done well for herself as an influencer and had her own channel where she promoted a cookware range that was also on sale at an elite shopping venue, Duchan Fayre.

'It all sounds amazing.' It felt strange but wonderful to slip into the Glenbriar gossip and Georgie could almost forget how long she'd been away. Life in tennis didn't seem to matter as much as everything that was going on here.

Hayley was getting married in three weeks to her fiancé, Oliver Wright. Georgie vaguely remembered him from school, though he was a bit older than them.

'Actually,' Hayley said, 'you should come to the wedding. There's plenty of space for the evening reception. Come for the dancing.'

The invitation caught Georgie off guard, but she instantly started planning her wardrobe in her head. 'Are you sure? I wouldn't want to impose.'

'Don't be daft.' Hayley waved away her concerns. 'You're back. We're celebrating. It makes perfect sense.'

'You better find a date.' Elise winked. 'Someone tall, dark, and handsome perhaps?'

Heat crept up Georgie's neck. 'I'm not sure where I'd find someone like that with such short notice. Or anyone, for that matter.'

'Mmm.' Elise raised an eyebrow. 'Not even your handsome mixed doubles partner?'

'Oh... him,' Georgie said.

Three pairs of eyes fixed on her.

'Kerr Halley,' Elise informed the others.

'But he's Jake's brother,' Hayley said, frowning. 'What even happened there? I know you dated, but—'

'We did.' Georgie fiddled with her teaspoon. 'I actually came back to apologise to Jake. The way we split up was a nightmare. But it was Kerr's house I ended up at. Accidentally. And then Amanda paired me with him for the mixed doubles. It was just a coincidence.' Though she was painfully aware how things had developed – in her mind anyway.

'Do tell,' Genevieve said.

Georgie smiled. What were friends for if not to share things like this with? She gave them a rundown of what had happened with her and Jake, plus her impromptu trip to Glasgow with Kerr, though through all of it, she carefully avoided mentioning how she was starting to feel about him. Facts were easier to recount.

'You were stuck in a landslip?' Hayley's eyes boggled. 'I saw stuff about that online.'

'Yeah, it was pretty scary.'

'Mental.' Genevieve shook her head. 'Thank goodness you were both ok.'

'My own silly fault for not wanting to drive on motorways.'

'You do you,' Hayley said. 'It's your call.'

'Kerr talked me into coming back via the main roads, and I managed it. So I feel more confident about doing it again another time.'

'Do you know about Kerr's ex?' Hayley sipped on her flat white.

Georgie shook her head. 'He didn't mention an ex.'

'They were together for nearly four years. Everyone thought they'd get married eventually.'

'What happened?'

'She got offered some big research position abroad... was it in Australia?' Hayley frowned.

The other two shook their heads, obviously not as up to speed on the gossip as Hayley.

'Anyway, wherever it was, she gave Kerr about a week's notice before she was gone.'

A small knot formed in Georgie's stomach. 'That's rough.'

'She didn't ask him to go with her or anything.' Hayley glanced around before continuing. 'And then the research grant fell through after she'd been there about three months. She came back and expected things to pick up where they left off.'

'And did they?' Georgie asked.

'Apparently so.'

'Kerr's a nice guy,' Elise said. 'I work with his mum, and she always says how sweet he is. I bet he gave his ex a second chance.'

'He did,' Hayley said. 'But then she got another offer, and she did it again. Total nightmare.'

Georgie's fingers tightened around her mug. 'Twice? She left him twice?'

She didn't ask how Hayley knew all this. Presumably from working in the hairdresser. Gossip was an everyday event in there.

'Yep. Poor guy.'

Wow, Kerr hadn't mentioned any of that. Not that she expected him to, but it shed a different light on him. She couldn't analyse it all here, but as soon as she was back in the peace of Heather Glen, she would. The Kerr Halley puzzle had just got even more intriguing.

Chapter Fourteen

Kerr

'You still reliving the weekend's near-death experience?' Eddie leaned forward and took a gingersnap from the open tin on the staffroom table.

Heat crept up Kerr's neck. 'Um... kind of.' His mind had strayed way too often to Georgie since the weekend. So much so, he'd almost forgotten the drama with the landslip. Still, it provided a good cover story for the moments when his brain left the building and skipped off to the campervan seeking Georgie. How crazy was it to think that fifteen or so years ago he'd been exactly like this, in this very building, and because of the exact same woman?

It was like being a fifteen-year-old with a crush all over again.

'Have you spoken to Amanda yet?' Eddie nibbled his biscuit.

'No, she messaged me saying we needed a meeting to discuss the meeting.'

Eddie laughed. 'Amanda loves her meetings.'

'Doesn't she just.'

Eddie peered at him with a half-raised eyebrow.

'What?'

'I've known you for a long time, and I know when you're not telling me something. What's eating you?'

Kerr shrugged. 'Just stuff, you know?' He was aware that Clara was listening. She was a kind person, and he didn't think she'd gossip, but he didn't feel like spilling his soul to an audience. Maybe if he had a chance to talk to Eddie on his own, but not here.

'Just stuff. It's nothing I want to talk about right now.'

'Ok.' Eddie patted his shoulder. 'I'll be here if you do.'

'Thanks, mate.' Kerr leaned over and touched the side of his head against Eddie's.

'I heard the road with the landslip is going to be closed indefinitely,' Clara said. 'It must have been really bad.'

Kerr rubbed the back of his neck. 'It was a narrow road, so I expect it'll be difficult to fix. We just got away as quickly as we could once we realised what had happened.'

'Were you on a day trip or something?' Clara smiled warmly at him, and he realised he hadn't elaborated on what he was doing. Only Eddie knew. Kerr wasn't sure he wanted the staffroom at large to know. Not when many of them would love the speculation.

'I, um... yeah. It was a tennis club thing,' he said vaguely.

At that moment, Mirren Elphinstone sat down next to Clara. She wore a floral dress over chunky boots, and her long golden hair flowing over her shoulders made her look more like she was dressed for a festival than school – though she was still perfectly smart. She just rocked the boho look more than most.

'Hey,' she said, looking at Kerr. 'The Autumn Gold Festival is only a couple of weeks away, and Benji was wondering if you were still able to help with the sound setup. The band would like to meet you.'

Kerr nodded. 'Yeah. I have a date to meet with Adam, the frontman. This week actually.'

'Ah... I think Adam and Benji have had a bit of a tiff. Reading between the lines. I don't get to see any of the backstage stuff. I've never even met the rest of the band. Benji likes to keep all that to himself.'

Except when he wanted her to pass on messages, it seemed. Kerr didn't voice that opinion, but he wondered if Mirren's cheery exterior hid something darker. She didn't look miffed about not being involved backstage with the band, but there was possibly something behind the bright eyes and the smile.

'Well, if he's there on Wednesday, I'll speak to both of them,' he said.

'Great.' Mirren smiled at him, then Eddie, then Clara. 'It all sounds amazing. Are any of you going to the gigs? Maybe we should have a staff night out.'

'I'm in for any night out,' Adele said, taking a seat. 'Where are we going?'

Kerr let the conversation continue around him, his mind drifting again. How the hell could he stop this from happening all the time?

'I mean it, Kerr,' Eddie whispered so only he could hear. 'Talk to me if something's bothering you.'

Kerr didn't have a chance to speak to Eddie about anything at school and, by the time he got home, he was too tired to message or call. And on Wednesday evening, he had the meeting with Tavrach to get through. Once again, he questioned why he kept volunteering for things, but then again, he always enjoyed them... Mostly. The landslip incident jumped to the front of his mind again. Weirdly, he *had* enjoyed that. Though for the wrong reasons.

Adam's house was on Golf Course Road, which did what it said on the tin and led straight to the course. Kerr had always liked this road. Half the houses looked like something from a Grand Designs offcut, the other half like they'd grown roots in the seventies and never bothered moving on – but in a charming sort of way. It was close to the tennis club, so he was familiar with it.

He strolled past a boxy glass-fronted new build, then an old stone bungalow with solar panels jammed on the roof at odd angles. Leaves skittered along the pavement in little gusts, catching at his ankles as he walked. Adam's place came into view a few houses down. Kerr had often seen this house without knowing who it belonged to. Its neatly trimmed front hedge was now tinged with gold, and the long driveway was carpeted with dark red leaves. The chunky garage looked like it could fit the entire band's equipment and then some. The house itself was a standard nineteen-seventies three-up-three-down, but the wide lawn and border of copper-leaved trees gave it a sense of space and quiet charm. Smoke drifted faintly from a nearby chimney. Kerr headed up the path, stepping over a conker that had split open on the drive. The unmistakable thump of bass and snare was already bleeding out from behind the garage doors. Band practice was in full swing.

He knocked on the side door, though the gesture seemed futile against the wall of sound. After a moment, he turned the handle and stepped inside.

The garage-turned-studio was a glorious contradiction of professional equipment nestled amid deliberate chaos. Cables snaked across the concrete floor like hungry serpents. Mismatched chairs formed a rough semicircle around a central performance area. Amplifiers of various vintages were stacked against one wall, while the other displayed a patchwork of band posters and setlists preserved in plastic sleeves.

The music stopped abruptly as a tall figure noticed his entrance. Kerr recognised Adam Cormack from years of following Tavrach. Adam silenced his guitar with a palm and nodded in

Kerr's direction. His dark hair was long and fell past his shoulders, and his arms were decorated with tattoos that disappeared beneath his band t-shirt. Rather incongruously, he had a pair of glasses perched atop his head, making him look more dad than danger.

'Hey,' he said in a low, rumbling voice. 'Are you Kerr?'

Kerr raised a hand in greeting. 'That's me.'

Adam's serious expression cracked into something closer to a smile. 'Great. Come in. Do you want a drink?'

'Um...'

'Tea or coffee? I'm not trying to get you pissed.'

Kerr laughed and shook his head. 'Thanks, but I'm ok.'

A younger man with tousled blond hair and a half smile stepped forward, hand extended. 'I'm Benji. Mirren's talked about you so much I feel like I know you already.'

'Likewise.' Kerr shook his hand, getting a strange sense that Benji was trying to silently crush his bones.

A short woman with a shock of purple hair and arms corded with muscle emerged from behind the drum kit. 'Hey.'

'This is Ailsa,' Adam said. 'Our rhythm section and resident critic.'

Ailsa wiped her hand on her jeans before offering it to Kerr. 'Someone has to maintain standards around here.'

From the keyboard setup in the corner, a slight man with wire-rimmed glasses raised a hand in greeting. 'Fergus,' he said simply. 'Don't mind Ailsa. She's just bitter because we voted against adding bagpipes to the bridge section.'

'I'm all for it,' Adam said. 'It was you boring ones who said no, so technically, it was a stalemate. Anyway...' he turned back to Kerr. 'Let me tell you the kind of thing we're looking for. It's not just Tavrach. It's the Autumn Gold Festival in general. But we headline there a lot, and I'm on the committee – for my sins. And I'm sure there are many of them.'

Kerr wasn't. Adam looked a bit intimidating, but he wasn't giving off scary vibes, and he was well-spoken and seemed almost gentle. Benji, on the other hand, had his arms folded and was watching Kerr with slightly narrowed eyes, though he still had a vague smile playing on his lips.

Adam gestured for Kerr to follow, weaving between amp stacks and a mic stand that looked like it had seen war. He pulled open a side door that led into a compact office space – more shelves of gear, a whiteboard, battered flight cases and, inexplicably, a lava lamp. Kerr stepped in, perching on the edge of a spare speaker cab.

'So...' Adam pulled a folded paper from his back pocket. 'We're doing five venues across the Autumn Gold week. I'm on sound duty for most of them. I need someone who knows what they're doing, isn't flaky, and doesn't vanish mid-gig to get "fresh air".' He made air quotes with a raised brow.

'No worries. I'm a teacher. I'm good at lurking,' Kerr said.

'It helps, doesn't it? I'm a college lecturer by day, so I get it.'

'What do you lecture in?'

'Music.' He grinned.

Kerr laughed. 'Figures.'

'Right, here's what we've got.' Adam flattened the paper onto the top of a bass amp. 'The Stagger Inn's running two nights. It's not exactly the Albert Hall, but they've got a half-decent PA if you can coax it. Problem is, the mixing desk's older than me and stuck behind the bar, so you need to shout over folk ordering pints while balancing gain levels. Fun.'

'Sounds like a laugh,' Kerr said dryly.

Adam cracked another grin. 'Oh, you'll love it. There's a tendency for sudden feedback when the mics get warm. I've tried convincing them to upgrade, but the landlord reckons it adds "authenticity".'

'Authenticity is code for tight-arsed,' Ailsa called from the other room.

'Exactly.' Adam flicked a finger in her direction. 'Then we've got The Pink Hotel.'

Kerr smirked. Everyone in Glenbriar knew the Loch View Hotel by its unofficial name – the one that coordinated with its paintwork.

Another door opened that presumably led into the house, and a teenage boy peered around. 'Dad, can I watch an eighteen?'

'No, you fecking can't. You're only seventeen, and it's a school night. Plus, your brother's in there, and he's only eleven.'

The boy looked at Kerr, and his eyes widened. 'Mr Halley.' He raised his hand, his cheeks going slightly pink.

'Hi, Greig.' Kerr wanted to laugh. He could only imagine how mortifying this must be for a kid to find his teacher here.

'There you go,' Adam said. 'Your teacher's here, so you better behave and do what you're told.' Adam looked around at Kerr. 'I hope he behaves in class.'

Kerr nodded. 'Yeah, he does.' In fact, he was a good kid. Always diligent, like worrying about missing lessons when he went to the dentist. Kerr had never made the connection between him and Adam.

'Bugger off for a bit,' Adam said. 'You can play the PlayStation for an hour as long as you let Robbie join in. And boil the kettle, will you? My tea's cold.' Adam handed him a white mug that had a black bowtie and the words Mr Sexy written on it. Greig took it, looking at it with disgust and also like he hoped the floor would swallow him whole.

'Students give me weird shit like that all the time,' Adam muttered as Greig headed out. Kerr was glad his students didn't. He'd be mortified if they did. It was bad enough when his colleague, the rather glamorous geography teacher, Brenna Bonham, told him she'd overheard kids saying he was the 'hottest teacher' and apparently they were now 'shipping' him with Miss Elphinstone. Kerr glanced at the door, very glad Benji didn't know that. Even if Kerr had never and would never look at Mirren like that, the idea made his stomach squirm at what her boyfriend might think.

'Where were we?' Adam ran his hands through his hair, dislodging his glasses. 'That's where they are.' He took them off and sat them beside a rather grubby looking laptop.

'The Pink Hotel.'

'Oh, yes.' Adam clicked his finger. 'So, it's got a function room that's a bit of an acoustic nightmare. Glass wall at the back, chandeliers above, and a polished floor. It bounces sound like nobody's business. So we need tight monitoring, clever mic placement, and someone who doesn't panic when the levels suddenly spike.'

'You're really selling it,' Kerr muttered, but he grinned.

'Last year,' Adam went on, 'someone tried to plug in a fog machine mid-set and tripped the breaker. Took down the lights, the amps, and the beer fridge. Near riot. I didn't think Briony would want us back. But she was ok about it.'

'Oh dear.'

'Yeah, so, basically,' Adam continued, undeterred, 'I'd need you to run the desk at both those venues, be on standby for the other gigs, and help us with the Saturday night slot at the Cross Keys. If the weather's good, we'll do it on the outside stage by the river. Covered, but still a nightmare for cables.'

Kerr nodded slowly. 'What kind of tech have you got? Digital or analogue desk?'

'Bit of both. We use a Behringer X32 rack for outdoor gigs, but the pub and hotel are old-school. You comfortable working with both?'

'Yeah. No worries.'

Adam's smirk returned. 'Sounds like you'll fit right in.'

Kerr hung about and chatted to the others for a while before saying goodbye and stepping out into the breeze and the fading light. The band kicked up again behind him, a muffled thrum of bass and snare following him as he walked. He zipped up his hoodie, hands deep in his pockets, brain already whirring with everything Adam had told him. The overload of information had certainly pushed Georgie out of his mind.

It was one thing helping out on the occasional gig, but this felt like something bigger. Proper organised chaos. He liked it. Adam seemed solid. Straight-talking. No bullshit. And the rest of the band seemed cool too. People always said never to meet your idols but meeting them hadn't soured Kerr's opinion of them. Only Benji gave off a weird vibe, but that might be because Kerr had a warped opinion of him after some of Mirren's comments.

He reached the end of the driveway and turned left, boots crunching over a line of dry leaves skittering along the pavement. Golf Course Road was quiet, the wind picking up and rustling the hedges. Most of the big houses here were set back from the street, behind low stone walls or modern render jobs with video doorbells and symmetrical pot plants. Lights flickered on inside. Warm rectangles of gold behind glass.

A movement caught his eye – someone crossing the garden of one of the older properties, chatting to a dog or a cat. He half recognised the voice, but it didn't register why until he heard his own name.

'Kerr?'

He turned slowly, peering past the low garden wall to see Amanda waving from the patio of one of the sleek new houses at the end of the street. Hers was part of a small cluster of large, architect-designed homes, all glass-fronted and sharp-edged, with landscaped gardens and smart driveways edged in granite setts. Autumn had softened the clean lines with drifts of golden leaves gathered against the fences and the crisp scent of woodsmoke in the air.

'I thought that was you!' She tugged a camel-coloured cashmere gilet tighter over her crisp white shirt, her breath visible in the cool air. A little dog trotted at her heels across the lawn. 'Have you been at the courts?'

'No.' Kerr gestured back towards Adam's house. 'I'm helping Tavrach with their sound setup for the festival.'

'Oh, do you know Adam? He's a good neighbour. Could be awkward with the music of course, but he's got good soundproofing. He helped out at a church do earlier in the year, which was super. That was how I got to know him. I had no idea we lived along the road from a rockstar. I'm on the festival committee this year too. Such a lot of juggling.'

Kerr waited for her to stop talking.

'Sounds... busy,' he said when she paused. She was worse than him for taking on all the committees.

'Frantic. But in the best way. And that reminds me, I've been meaning to catch you about the MUGA project. I've finally got some space in my diary.' She pulled out her phone. 'How about tomorrow, around four-thirty? David's off in the afternoon, he can have the kids.'

'Tomorrow?' Kerr repeated. Just what he wanted straight after school, but maybe it was better than having it hanging over him for another time. 'Yeah. Ok.'

'Perfect, see you tomorrow then. And don't worry about dinner. I'll cook something.'

'Thanks.'

Kerr had a good excuse to leave work sharp on Thursday afternoon, though he wasn't sure spending time with Amanda would be any better than staying late with a heap of marking.

Amanda's kitchen looked like it had been transplanted directly from an interior design magazine – all gleaming marble surfaces, country-style cupboard fronts, and an AGA cooker that probably cost more than Kerr's annual salary.

Georgie sat at the far end of the kitchen table in a thick cream jumper with her hair loose and trailing over her shoulders. She smiled as Amanda showed him in. He tried to return it, but his insides were behaving very strangely, and he felt over warm – probably because of that bloody AGA.

'Right.' Amanda settled at the head of the table with her phone in one hand and a leather-bound notebook in the other. 'Tell me everything about the Glasgow meeting.'

What followed was less a debriefing and more of an enthusiastic interrogation, with Amanda jotting notes and occasionally interjecting with her own strategic suggestions. Kerr spoke on autopilot, his conscious attention continually drawn to Georgie.

She spoke with her hands, her elegant, expressive fingers giving shape to her words. On her left index finger, she wore a ring – not dissimilar to the one he wore, only hers was less chunky and more feminine. He rubbed his own ring as he listened. 'And I made lots of notes.' She pulled out a book of her own.

As she laid it on the table, their eyes met for a moment too long, and heat burned the back of his neck. Amanda glanced between them, then focused on Georgie as she went through the notes.

'Well,' Amanda said, 'you two certainly make a formidable team.' Her phone chimed with an elaborate ringtone. She glanced at the screen and stood abruptly. 'I need to take this – it's the festival committee treasurer. Back in five.' She swept from the room in a cloud of expensive perfume, her voice already shifting to her phone tone as she disappeared down the hallway.

The sudden silence felt weighty.

'How have you been?' Georgie asked. 'Since the... adventure?'

'Fine,' Kerr said automatically. 'Busy. You?'

She smiled, and really, she was very beautiful with even teeth and glossy pink lips. She fiddled with her ring and Kerr found himself mirroring the action. 'Same. I've met up with some old friends. That kind of thing.'

Kerr gave a slow nod. He wanted to ask how long she was planning on staying, but that sounded like a loaded question… and perhaps a bit rude.

But as their eyes met again, his heart flickered in his chest, and he couldn't deny what was happening in there. He was falling for Georgie Porter. Jake's ex. The woman he'd spent years resenting on his brother's behalf.

Oh Christ.

This was bad. He was smitten. And he had absolutely no idea what to do about it.

Chapter Fifteen

Georgie

Georgie slid her chair back as Amanda began gathering up the crockery. The meeting had drifted into dinner. Amanda's version of 'something simple' turned out to be coq au vin with dauphinoise potatoes and a side of roasted fennel. She was truly a domestic goddess. Georgie knew she'd never be anything like this. How Amanda managed three kids, a dog, a house this size, and all the committees she was on was jaw dropping.

'I'll help with these.' Georgie reached for the plates.

'Absolutely not,' Amanda replied briskly. 'I'll load the dishwasher. You two have done all the hard work. Would you like dessert or coffee?'

Georgie caught Kerr's eye. He gave a small smile and stood, pushing his chair in neatly. 'Not for me, thanks,' he said. 'Though I don't mind loading up. It's a novelty for me. My kitchen is too small for a dishwasher.'

'I'm full too, thanks.' Georgie got to her feet too. 'That was so tasty.'

'Well, it was lovely to see you.' Amanda beamed at them both. 'And thank you. I feel much more confident about the MUGA application now.'

'Thanks for dinner.' Kerr gave her a pat on the arm.

Amanda waved them off. As the front door shut behind them, the quiet of the evening settled in. A breeze lifted Georgie's hair and carried the faint scent of woodsmoke from a nearby chimney.

'Can I give you a lift?' She nodded towards her campervan parked at the bottom of Amanda's drive. It wasn't far for Kerr to walk, but it felt strange not to offer when she'd be passing that way anyway.

He hesitated. 'Um, ok,' he said at last. 'As long as you stick to actual roads this time. Preferably the kind without recent landslips.'

Georgie burst out laughing. 'Spoilsport.'

He gave her a sidelong glance, a smile twitching at the corners of his mouth. 'I'm traumatised. Don't make me relive it.'

'I thought you rather enjoyed it.'

'What makes you say that?'

'Intuition.' She unlocked the van and climbed in.

He followed, pulling the passenger door shut with a solid clunk.

The drive through Glenbriar's quiet streets was brief, the van's headlights cutting through the darkness as they wound towards Kirk Lane. Raised on a hill next to it was the very picturesque little church, lit up like a service was on.

'Here you go.' Georgie pulled up outside Kerr's house.

'Thanks.' Kerr paused, his eyes lingering on her for a moment. 'You can come in for a bit if you want.'

She held his gaze, and it was easy to tell it wasn't a throwaway request or a rhetorical question. If anything, he was looking at her like he wanted her to say yes. Did that mean he had an agenda? Perhaps to talk about Jake?

'I'd like that,' she said before she could overthink it anymore. The other option was to drive back to Heather Glen and spend the rest of the evening on her own.

'Cool.' He led the way inside.

The house was very quaint on the outside, like something out of an old storybook with tiny windows and a quirky little doorstep. Inside, it didn't feel much bigger than the van, though it clearly had more rooms, but none of them were exactly large.

'Take a seat.' He pushed open the door to the living room. A sofa and a TV dominated the room, but it also had a small table with a laptop on it and a bookshelf. 'What would you like to drink? I could do hot chocolate. Seems like that kind of night, but I've got tea, coffee—'

'Hot chocolate sounds perfect.' She settled on the sofa as he went into another room. Leaning her head back, she listened as the kettle boiled and mugs clattered.

'Here you go.' Kerr returned with two mugs and placed one on a tiny end table next to Georgie. He sat at the other end of the sofa, cradling his own mug.

'Why do you wear that ring?' she asked. 'Does it have significance?'

'Not really. I just like it.'

'It's nice.' She held up her own. 'It's a bit like mine, isn't it?' Holding it alongside his, they compared them. His index finger was considerably larger than hers, but the ring designs looked like they could have come from a 'his and hers' set.

'Very like. Why did you get yours?'

'Same reason.' She took a sip of hot chocolate. 'I just liked it.'

He caught her eye and smiled. 'If you hadn't had the shoulder injury, would you have carried on playing tennis?'

She shook her head. 'I don't know. I guess I couldn't have gone on forever. But I suppose I thought after the surgery on my shoulder, things would improve, and it's fine doing day-to-day things, but obviously when you're hitting shots and serves every day, it takes its toll. It was hard to keep up with the younger players.' She hugged her mug. 'And even some of the ones my age. My form dropped after the surgery. It's easy to blame it on the shoulder, but it might have happened anyway. Tennis isn't exactly a long-term career.'

'So what will you do? Go into commentary?'

She sipped more of the creamy hot chocolate to stall for time. He'd hit on the question she didn't know the answer to. 'Possibly. I need time away for a bit. Life has been full on for a long time.'

He nodded, still with his eyes on her.

'Playing tennis is really stressful. Particularly the singles tournaments. There are thousands of people watching you, millions more on TV, and yet you're completely alone out there.'

'Teaching's the opposite, in a way. Never a moment alone, surrounded by people all day.'

'But that's its own kind of lonely, isn't it?' She raised an eyebrow. 'Being the one responsible for so many others.'

Their eyes met in a moment of understanding, and a little door unlocked in her chest. A secret place she hardly ever let anyone into, but Kerr had stumbled on the key, and if he invaded now, she'd let him in.

The minutes dissolved as they talked about everything and nothing, though carefully skirting around mentions of Jake. Kerr got up at one point and refilled their hot chocolates. When he came back, they chatted about funny things that had happened on the tour or in Kerr's classes.

'Honestly, it was so funny.' Laughter lines creased his beautiful face, and Georgie saw the real Kerr shining through. Not the guarded man he usually was around her.

The whole evening had passed without a mention of Jake.

'Christ.' Kerr grabbed his phone and jolted upright.

'What's wrong?' Georgie stared at him.

'It's nearly midnight.'

'What?' How the hell had they talked that long?

Georgie laughed and uncurled herself from the end of the sofa. 'I'm so sorry. I had no idea it was so late.'

'No, no, it's fine.' He gathered their mugs. 'I don't know where the time went.'

She got up, still smiling. 'Thanks for the chat... and the hot chocolates. It was fun.'

At the door, they paused, slightly awkward again.

'Well, see you about,' Kerr said finally. 'And thanks for staying. It was... nice. To talk.'

'It was.' Georgie reached out and gently touched his arm. A powerful urge to wrap her arms around him and hug him surged through her, but she ignored it, breathing through it, just like she did when shooting pains ripped through her shoulder before a second serve. 'See you.'

She stepped into the cool night air, acutely aware of him watching from the doorway as she walked to her van. Only when she'd started the engine did he finally close his door, the warm light from within disappearing like a snuffed candle.

She'd never had a night quite like that. Years in the spotlight, all the interviews and press conferences, all the superficial conversations with other players and coaches and the endless parade of people who wanted proximity to her success were so far removed from the simple pleasure of just chatting without an agenda, a performance or properly maintained barriers.

She took the turn towards Heather Glen. She'd had chats with friends of course – even the recent meeting with Hayley, Elise, and Genevieve was a good chinwag, but it hadn't been like this.

If things were different – if the past was less complicated, if Jake wasn't a factor – what might be possible between her and Kerr?

But Jake was a factor. He would always be a factor. His hurt, his anger, his claim on both their loyalties stood between them like a twenty-foot wall, and she couldn't see a way of either climbing it, or knocking it down.

By Sunday afternoon, the sky had settled into that washed-out grey that made everything look a bit damp even when it wasn't raining. A faint chill clung to the air, woodsmoke coiled from a nearby chimney, and leaves blew across the tarmac as Georgie turned into the Fairways Estate. It was a new development that hadn't existed when she'd lived here before, with sweeping drives, mock-stone facades, and precision-trimmed hedges flanking the wide road. Amber and russet ivy snaked through the ornamental trees planted along the verge, and a few pumpkins decorated front steps as Halloween was approaching.

Hayley's house was near the end of the road, a double-fronted building with pristine windows and a glass door.

Georgie parked behind Elise's car on the large driveway and spotted Genevieve's little electric car already tucked in next to the wooden bin tidy. She grabbed her bag and headed for the front step just as the door opened.

'Hey.' Hayley stood framed in the doorway in black leggings and a pink top that read *Bride Mode: Activated*. 'Come in.'

Georgie smiled. 'Love the top.'

'Genevieve gave me it. Fun, isn't it?'

The interior was as impressive as the exterior – open-plan and modern, with gleaming hardwood floors and expensive looking furniture. Through the archway to the kitchen, Georgie spotted a tall man in a crisp white shirt, his back to them as he poured something into a glass.

'This is Oliver,' Hayley said. 'He and Finlay are going out in a minute; they're hiding from the wedding talk.' She glanced around. 'And Finlay's probably hiding from Elise... The joys of having an ex who's friends with his wife.'

'Oops.'

As if on cue, another man came into the kitchen. Even if Georgie hadn't vaguely remembered him from school, she would have recognised him as Hayley's brother; they had similar eyes and smiles.

'Right. I've said goodbye to the dear wife.' Finlay spotted Georgie and raised an eyebrow. 'Ah, you're the famous lady who's been working with Kerr on the MUGA funding, aren't you?'

She gave a smile. 'Um... Yes.'

'I work with him. I'm a P.E. teacher, so the MUGA is close to my heart too. I work with the junior rugby team, and we have some input for the funding committee.'

'That's good. Because at the meeting I was at with Kerr, they suggested the more groups that were involved, the better.'

'Absolutely. I've got a meeting with Amanda next week.'

Georgie smiled, knowing how delighted Amanda would be about that. Meetings were her catnip.

Oliver gave Georgie a brief smile before he dropped a kiss on Hayley's cheek, then he and Finlay headed off.

'The others are in the conservatory.' Hayley led Georgie through the house, to the extension filled with potted plants and wicker furniture. Elise sat cross-legged on the floor, surrounded by tiny tulle bags and silvery ribbons, her sleek dark hair falling forward as she concentrated on tying perfect bows. Genevieve occupied the largest armchair, cradling her baby bump.

'How are you?' Genevieve asked.

'Good. Thanks for inviting me.'

'Hayley's got us on a production line.'

'My other two bridesmaids, Lilah and Willow, can't make it.' Hayley smiled at Georgie. 'You'll meet them at the wedding. Lilah is married to my cousin, and Willow is my cousin on the other side of my family.'

'Do you just know everyone?' Laughter bubbled from Georgie's chest.

'I do.' Hayley nodded with half a frown as if trying to think of someone she didn't know.

'Thanks for inviting me when I'm not even a bridesmaid.'

'No worries. I've got Ophelia coming too. She's a friend who's not a bridesmaid either. But she's an interior designer, so she's great at making things match.'

Georgie kicked off her shoes and settled on the floor beside Elise, accepting the heap of organza circles and silver-wrapped almonds pushed her way.

'The wedding's in three weeks, and I'm feeling the pressure now,' Hayley said.

'All this for one day,' Elise said with a theatrical sigh.

'Says the woman who's already planning a wedding to a man she's been dating for five minutes.' Genevieve winked.

'Who said anything about getting married?' Elise's cheeks coloured slightly.

'It's obvious.' Genevieve exchanged a look with Georgie, and they both giggled.

The easy banter and comfortable teasing was something she'd missed during her years away. These girlfriend groups with no secret competition or rivalry were such fun.

'Have you found any hotties to bring to the wedding?' Hayley asked, pulling Georgie from her thoughts.

'Um... no...' Heat rushed to Georgie's cheeks, and she focused intently on tying a particularly tricky bow. This really was like being a teenager again, but all she could think about was Kerr. He was the only person she would want with her. But he'd never agree.

'Oh my god.' Genevieve leaned forward. 'Does this mean you have someone in mind?'

'Kind of.'

'Really?' Hayley sat back on her heels and stared.

Georgie hesitated, then sighed. 'You remember Kerr?'

'How could we forget?' Hayley's brown eyes were wide. 'Did something happen in the campervan the night you two got stranded?'

Georgie shook her head, though how could she forget how good it had been cuddled up in his arms? 'Not really. But I like him.' She gave a helpless shrug.

'Even though he's Jake's brother?' Elise's eyebrows rose towards her hairline.

'Yeah.' Georgie looked back at the favour. 'And there lies the problem.'

'Look,' Hayley said, 'Jake stuff aside, Kerr's a good guy.'

'Finlay says the same,' Genevieve added. 'They seem to get on great at work.'

'I know he's all these things, but that doesn't help. How can I ask out my ex's brother?'

Elise covered her face. 'You're asking the person who's now dating her ex's best friend and whose own friend is now married to her other ex.' She grinned at Genevieve.

'Yeah, I get that. I'm just not sure it's a road Kerr would go down, even if I wanted to.'

'I get it,' Hayley said. 'And maybe in this case, you'd be better staying away. Which makes me sad because I'm a hopeless romantic... Still, I always say, you never know until you try.'

Indeed. That was true. And if she asked him and the whole situation blew up, she could always just vanish from the scene of the crime. It wasn't like she truly belonged in Glenbriar anyway, was it?

Chapter Sixteen

Kerr

October

'She said it's all looking promising.' Finlay plonked a laden plate onto the staffroom table. Kerr was always amazed at how he seemed to sweet talk the dinner ladies into giving him extra helpings.

'I think if we all work together, we've got a good chance of success.' Kerr took a seat opposite Finlay, beside Brenna, the effortlessly glam geography teacher who somehow made sleek leggings and a long sweater look like designer wear. Her dark, glossy hair was pinned back in a loose knot, a pair of gold hoops catching the light as she huddled in beside Clara, quietly conferring. Clara glanced up and smiled at Kerr.

'We have a real need for the MUGA here,' he continued to Finlay. 'There are so many groups that would use it.'

'Definitely.' Finlay took a mouthful of pasta and seemed to almost swallow it whole. 'It's actually long overdue. Amanda seems exactly the right person to get the job done.'

'Yeah, she's hoping to fast-track the application. She's on a mission.'

Finlay huffed a laugh. 'Isn't she always? I used to be engaged to her sister-in-law. I'm glad I got out of it – not only because I'm happy I married Genevieve, but I dodged Amanda as an extended family member. Lovely as she is, she can be intense.'

'She sure can.'

Finlay leaned back in his chair. 'I bumped into Georgie Porter the other day. You know her, don't you?'

Kerr's brows tugged together, and he had an odd feeling that, although Brenna was still talking to her, Clara was listening to his and Finlay's discussion. 'Er... Yeah.'

'She was at my sister's house, making up wedding favours.' Finlay grinned. 'Oliver and I buggered off for a cycle run.'

'Weren't you helping?' Kerr raised an eyebrow.

'These hands were not made for delicate work like that.' Finlay held them up to demonstrate. 'But we've done lots of other jobs, so it's all good. Georgie's very normal for someone who's famous, though maybe that's just my misconception of what "normal" is.'

'Right.' Kerr unclipped his lunchbox, still with a sense that Clara had been watching him but had quickly returned her gaze to Brenna when he looked over. 'I guess normal is relative... And are any of us really normal?'

Finlay chuckled. 'No, probably not.'

'Speak for yourself.' Adele sat down next to Finlay with a sigh, unclipping her lunchbox with her long nails. 'Some days I question my life choices,' she said. 'God knows who thought becoming deputy head would be a promotion. I feel like I've been sent to the front line some days. And it's not the kids. It's the parents who are the worst offenders.'

'I'll try to be good when the baby arrives.' Finlay grinned at her.

'You better be.'

Kerr shook his head, smiling at them, but his attention was pulled away by the angry buzzing of his phone on the table.

'Excuse me. I've got to take this.' Jake's name was flashing on the screen along with his picture – even that looked a bit grumpy.

Kerr got up and stood beside the door. Eddie was on his way in with Gil Warden, the headteacher, and Sam Addison, the English teacher.

'Jake,' he answered.

Eddie patted Kerr's shoulder on the way past.

'Is everything ok?' Kerr continued, watching Eddie sit down beside Adele. Sam took a seat next to Clara and leaned in to speak to her. She laughed and shook her head.

'No, it's not.' Jake's voice was tight. 'I just got off the phone with Mum, and she told me that Georgie is apparently still hanging around Glenbriar. She's been meeting old friends and doesn't seem in any rush to go away. Mum works with one of them.'

Kerr closed his eyes, pressing his thumb and forefinger against the bridge of his nose. Had Georgie told these friends about their campervan 'adventure'? If she had, what if it got back to his mum? Christ. He'd have to speak to his mum and think up a good cover story. Or did she already know?

'Have you seen her again?' Jake asked. 'Since that day you were out with her?'

'She's still helping on the MUGA project.'

'So is that a yes?'

'Yes… I have to go to the meetings, so I can't really avoid her.'

'What's she playing at?'

'I don't think she's playing at anything,' Kerr said quietly. 'I think she's just trying to figure out what's next. The tour wasn't—'

'Oh, don't even go there,' Jake cut in. 'Are you seriously defending her? After everything? After what she did?'

'I'm not defending what happened,' Kerr said. 'I'm just saying people are complicated. Situations are complicated.'

'She's not complicated, Kerr. She's selfish. Always has been. She uses people until they're not useful anymore, then moves on without a backward glance. She always does this. Everyone gets sucked in. Then spat out when she's had her fill.'

'That's not fair, Jake,' he said. 'She came back because—'

'Oh my god,' Jake interrupted. 'You're actually buying it. Whatever sob story she's selling, you're right there with your wallet open.'

'It's not like that.'

'I know exactly what it's like. What it was like for years. She screwed me over, and now she's trying to get to you. Well, you take care. I don't want to see you hurt the way I was.'

The concern beneath the anger only made Kerr feel worse. 'I won't be.' Though he knew that was a lie. He might well be hurt – just not in the same way Jake had been.

The uncomfortable truth settled around him like dust: he'd fallen for Georgie Porter. On some level, he'd always fancied her. But what was he supposed to do about it?

If Jake was this angry just about Georgie being back in town, how would he react if he found out the truth about Kerr's feelings?

There was only one option: make sure he didn't find out. No one could.

Kerr zipped his jacket to the collar and stepped out into the crisp afternoon air. The tennis club was twenty minutes from his house if he took the direct route, but he had a detour in mind. One he'd been putting off all week.

The thought of it had been sitting in the back of his head since his call with Jake. If Georgie's friends had told his mum about the 'campervan mishap', he needed to make sure she didn't get the wrong idea... Or possibly the right idea – just the one Jake couldn't ever find out.

He adjusted the strap of his tennis bag and crossed over at the junction, heading up the hill to Arden Crescent where he'd grown up.

The nineteen seventies and eighties houses on this street had kept well, and this was considered a very good part of the town to live in. His parents' house looked the same as it always had, except for the conservatory they'd added later, and how the garden had grown up around it.

He exhaled, squared his shoulders, and went up to the front door. His mum opened it before he had a chance to knock. She held her phone in one hand. 'I saw you coming up the path. How are you, Kerr Bear?'

'I'm good. Just passing.' He gave her a hug. 'Mind if I come in for a minute?'

'Course not, my love. Dad's in the conservatory. Come on through.'

She stepped aside, and he followed her into the hallway. The house was always neat and tidy but lived-in, rather than show home.

Douglas looked up from the sofa as Kerr came through, one arm slung along the back, feet up, glass of orange juice in hand.

'Ah, hullo, son. What you doing here?'

'I'm just on my way to the tennis club. Thought I'd stop by.'

Kate narrowed her eyes slightly, a faint crease forming between her brows. 'Is everything all right?'

He nodded. 'Well, mostly. I just wanted to set something straight before it gets twisted.'

Now he had their full attention. Douglas put his glass down and leaned forward.

Kerr adjusted the strap of his tennis bag. 'You might've heard already, or you might hear, something about me spending time with Georgie Porter.'

Kate raised an eyebrow. 'I haven't. Should I have?'

'Well, you work with her friend. So I thought she might've said something.'

Kate gave a slight shrug. 'She didn't. Well, she told me Georgie was back in town. But go on. Why have you been spending time with her?'

Kerr exhaled through his nose. 'She's been helping with the MUGA funding application. Amanda asked her to get involved because of her tennis contacts.'

'Right.'

'There was a meeting in Glasgow a couple of weeks ago,' he went on, trying to sound as casual as possible. 'Amanda couldn't go, so she pretty much volunteered Georgie and me. But on the way back, we got caught in that landslip near Strathbeck and we had to stay overnight in her campervan.'

Kate's expression sharpened, her eyes narrowing. 'A landslip? You didn't mention that.'

'I didn't want to make a big deal of it. We were fine, and we got back the next morning.'

Kate folded her arms. 'You got stranded in a landslip and didn't think to tell us?'

'I didn't want it to sound worse than it was.'

Douglas gave a low whistle. 'Bet it takes them years to fix that road like it did with the one here when you were wee.'

'Yeah. I expect so.' He watched his mum, who looked like she was puzzling something out.

'It's just...' he started again, 'I didn't want folk jumping to conclusions. She's got history here. And with Jake obviously. I didn't ask for this. It's all been sort of – thrust on me.'

Kate's gaze softened, but she let out a sigh. 'She's something else, isn't she? I'm not sure I like her swanning back now that it suits her and getting her name behind big projects like she's always been part of this town, when really she hasn't.'

'It's not like that,' Kerr said.

Douglas raised his eyebrows. 'Sounds like she's looking for a cause since her career ended and she's found her way back here.'

'And I suppose everyone will welcome her with open arms.'

'And why shouldn't they?' Kerr adjusted his grip on his bag. 'She hasn't hurt the whole town. She's sorry about what happened with Jake, and she wants to apologise. That's why she came here in the first place, but he didn't want to hear it.' Kerr gave them a helpless look. 'She told me the whole story, but I can't accept the apology on Jake's behalf. I believe she was sincere though. Why would she bother otherwise?'

'Why wouldn't Jake listen?' Kate said.

'Because you know what he's like.' Kerr shook his head. 'I think he needs professional help.'

'We offered him that before, but he wouldn't take it. It's a pity this can of worms has been opened again.' Kate rubbed her forehead.

Kerr sometimes wondered if Jake had ongoing mental health issues that he let fester because he was too proud to get help. But how could you force someone into it?

'I hope she moves on and leaves Jake alone,' Douglas said. 'I wish her no ill will, but I don't think any reunion with Jake is a sensible one. Maybe she wants it for her own peace of mind. But I feel like it'll just cause more trouble. Maybe you could tell her that if you see her again?'

'Yeah, ok.' Kerr sighed.

'Such a shame she chose to come back now, when there were all those years Jake would have loved her to come back, and she only did it once.'

Kerr gave a small nod. Yep. That one time at Jake's graduation and Kerr would never forget it. How could he? The spark had been so strong, and even now it hadn't died like it should have. *Thou shouldn't covet thy brother's ex-girlfriend...* But hell, Kerr had never managed that. 'I better go. I've got a match.'

'I hope your tennis partner's more straightforward than your social life,' Douglas muttered, though he was grinning.

'Well, it's Eddie, so let's hope.'

'Ha, good old Ed. Though he's old enough to be my mate, not yours.'

Kerr snorted. 'Don't I know it?'

He gave them both hugs, then carried on towards the club. He'd said what he needed to say. But guilt burned in his chest like slow-moving lava. Because no matter what story he told, the truth wasn't going anywhere.

The club was lively despite the season winding down and Kerr searched around for Eddie, but his eye was drawn to court three where Georgie knelt at eye level with a little girl – one of Amanda's kids – demonstrating a proper grip on a junior racket. Her hair was pulled back in a tight ponytail as per her usual tennis look. She wore navy tight leggings and a white polo shirt – nothing special, nothing flashy – but she still looked every inch the pro. The child nodded seriously at whatever Georgie was saying, then attempted a forehand that sent the ball skittering harmlessly into the net. Georgie encouraged her to try again.

Everyone gets sucked in.

Jake's voice replayed in Kerr's mind. He watched as Georgie high-fived the little girl for her next attempt. Was this everyone getting sucked in? Or was this a genuine effort on her part?

Georgie looked up, and her eyes landed on him. Her face brightened with a smile so genuine it seemed to light her from within, and she waved. Kerr's feet moved before his brain had fully processed the decision.

'Hi,' she said. 'How are you?'

'I'm fine. Have you seen Eddie?'

She shook her head. 'I don't think he's here yet. Do you want to hit some balls with me while you wait?' Her left eyebrow rose slightly as she said it, then she laughed. 'You have no idea what mileage we got out of ball jokes on the tour.'

'I bet.' He gave her a little smile. 'But, yeah, ok. Let's go crack balls.'

'That sounds even worse.'

They headed across the court and Kerr put his bag down on the bench next to the fence. 'I just saw my parents,' he said. 'We were talking about Jake... and you.'

'Oh?'

'Yeah. They think it might be a good idea if you don't bother apologising to him and let it go.'

'Ok... Fair enough. I just hate how I left it.'

'I get that, but...' Kerr ran his hands through his hair. 'Sometimes I think Jake has undiagnosed issues. My parents think so too, but he doesn't want to be helped. So people end up treading on eggshells around him. We're all worried that he'll have some big flare up if he's expecting you to turn up.'

She sucked on the knuckle of her thumb, then nodded. 'That makes sense. And of course I don't want to make him anxious. I didn't really think about it like that.'

'Thank you.' Kerr gently put his hand on her upper arm.

She looked up and smiled at him. 'I've been meaning to ask you something.' Glancing around, she fiddled with her racquet.

Kerr turned towards her, suddenly aware of how the sunlight was catching the gold flecks in her eyes, making them sparkle. 'What about?'

'Well, I was thinking—' she began, then stopped as someone called her name from through the fence. 'Oh, hi, Elise.' She started chatting to her friend as Kerr unpacked his racquet.

A hand clapped him on the back, and he turned to see Eddie. 'Sorry, I'm a bit late. I was helping Kenneth with the leaf blower. Silly contraptions really.'

Kerr smirked. He couldn't imagine Eddie getting on well with a leaf blower. He was probably delighted to have an excuse to get away.

Georgie turned back to them. When she saw Eddie, her expression flickered.

'Hi.' She gave him a little wave. 'Elise was telling me about a music festival her boyfriend is playing in.'

'The Autumn Gold Festival,' Kerr said.

'That's the one. Do you know it?'

'Everyone here knows it.' Eddie patted her arm gently. 'You really have been away a long time.'

'Oh gosh, I have, haven't I? It sounds like a lot of fun.'

'It's great,' Kerr said. 'I'm helping with sound this year. The local band Tavrach are playing, and their frontman is one of the festival organisers. You should come along to one of the gigs. They're always good.'

Georgie's expression brightened. 'I might do that.' She tightened the band in her hair. 'I could go with Elise if she's there to see her boyfriend.'

A surge of something suckered him in the gut. The thought that she might be at the gigs buoyed him up. With Eddie here now, he had no need to hit balls with Georgie, but as he walked to the far end of the court, he remembered she'd been on the verge of asking him something when Elise had called her over.

What was it?

With so many people here, there was no way of returning to the conversation. He slammed a serve down the line, and Eddie clapped his racquet. 'Great serve.'

'Thanks.' But his insides burned with curiosity. Still, he had to convince himself she'd only wanted to ask him something mundane, because what else could it be?

It wasn't like she was about to propose or anything. The thought made him laugh – right as he sent a shot straight into the net. Typical. That was how it felt about the whole situation with Georgie: a burst of momentum, then a crash into the mesh, his desires hurtling forward only to rebound in his face the second it looked like he might be getting somewhere. He didn't want his heart broken again. He'd invested a lot in getting over his horrible double breakup with Anna – returned to his hometown, made new friends. Yes, he wanted a relationship, but while Georgie appealed on so many levels, maybe choosing someone who didn't make his life so complicated would be better – and also choosing someone he knew for sure would stick around.

Chapter Seventeen

Georgie

The Stagger Inn throbbed with life, music pulsing through ancient floorboards as Georgie followed Elise through the packed entrance. Bodies pressed together, chatting, laughing and dancing. Some faces turned just for a moment to clock their arrival, and a few people obviously recognised Georgie. She kept her smile fixed in place, the same expression she'd perfected for post-match interviews and sponsorship events, though her stomach tightened a little with each new pair of eyes that lingered a beat too long.

'God, it's heaving in here,' Elise shouted over the noise, her emerald dress catching the light as she edged between clusters of festival-goers. 'Gabe said they'd be packed, but this is mental.'

Georgie nodded. This place always had a bit of a dodgy reputation, though Elise assured her it had moved on a lot after a change of ownership a few years back. Georgie's rust-coloured jacket felt a little too warm, the black camisole beneath clinging slightly to her skin.

'There's a table.' Elise grabbed her arm, pointing towards a small space near the makeshift stage. 'Come on. Before someone else gets it.'

They wove their way across the room. Georgie spotted Genevieve at a corner table, her pregnant belly prominently displayed beneath a flowing dress, one hand resting protectively on the curve while she laughed with her husband and another couple.

'That's Genevieve's brother with his girlfriend,' Elise said, following Georgie's gaze.

Genevieve waved them over. 'Hey. It's wild, isn't it?'

'What an atmosphere,' Georgie said. 'You look amazing, by the way.'

'I look like I swallowed a beach ball,' Genevieve laughed, rubbing her bump. 'But thank you.'

Across the room, Georgie saw Hayley with a group she recognised as her colleagues from the salon, plus an older woman with the same sharp cheekbones – Hayley's mum, she realised with a jolt of recognition.

Elise had already sat down at the tiny table.

'If you guard it, I'll get us drinks,' Georgie said.

As she weaved her way towards the bar, a middle-aged woman with carefully highlighted hair and an expression of barely contained excitement stepped up to her, clutching a glass of white wine.

'I hope you don't mind,' she said loudly, 'but I just had to come over. I followed your whole career. I never missed a match if I could help it. Such a shame what happened with your shoulder. You were brilliant. Still are, I'm sure.'

Georgie smiled. 'That's very kind, thank you.'

'My daughter plays, you know. Not at your level, of course, but she's got potential. Maybe someday...' the woman trailed off.

'That's wonderful,' Georgie said.

'Are you staying long in the town? Maybe you could do some coaching.'

'I haven't decided yet.'

The woman lingered, seemingly waiting for more, then retreated with a slightly disappointed nod when Georgie offered nothing further. She'd barely gone when an older man took her place, eager to recount watching her junior matches 'before you were anybody.'

Georgie nodded, smiled and thanked him before pushing her way to the bar and getting the drinks. By the time she returned to the table with two cocktails, she felt like she'd completed an obstacle course.

'You don't owe them your time,' Elise said. 'Just say you're here to enjoy the music.'

'It's fine,' Georgie replied. 'They were being nice.'

But when more people approached them, it got less and less fine. With each approach, each congratulation tinged with pity, each assessment of her career's premature end, she felt less like a person and more like an exhibit. The Fallen Champion, presented for your viewing pleasure. Observe how gracefully she accepts your condolences. Marvel at her polite smile as you dissect her failures.

Perhaps worse were some who didn't approach but huddled in corners, glancing her way with undisguised curiosity, whispering behind their hands. Georgie had spent most of her life being watched, but this hit different.

'Drink.' Elise pushed the cocktail closer. 'Doctor's orders.'

Georgie obediently took a sip, the sweet-sour liquid coating her tongue. 'It's strong.'

'That's rather the point.' Elise clinked her own glass against Georgie's. 'To surviving public scrutiny with your dignity intact.'

The lights dimmed slightly, signalling the beginning of the performances. Georgie settled back in her chair, allowing herself to breathe properly for the first time since entering. Around them, the pub continued its cheerful hum, dozens of conversations flowing like tributaries into a river of sound. She'd survived press conferences, post-match analyses, and the brutal scrutiny of social media. She could survive one night of Glenbriar nosiness.

The buzz of conversation faded as Gabriel Wilder, Elise's ruggedly handsome boyfriend, took the stage, acoustic guitar cradled against his chest. He was all quiet confidence with thoughtful eyes, and dressed in a linen shirt with rolled sleeves, dark jeans worn thin at the knees, and thick boots.

Beside Georgie, Elise straightened imperceptibly, her fingers stilling around her glass.

'Hey, folks,' Gabe spoke into the microphone, his voice a warm rumble. 'This is a new one. Still finding its feet, like most of us.' A ripple of appreciative laughter followed, the audience already won over before he'd played a single note.

Then he began to play, and the pub fell completely silent.

The melody was haunting – a gentle river of notes that built slowly, gaining depth and momentum with each measure. His fingers moved deftly across the strings, coaxing something achingly beautiful from wood and wire. When he began to sing, his voice held the room captive – not through technical perfection, but through raw emotion that seemed to reach directly into the chest of every listener.

The lyrics spoke of ancient stones and flowing waters, of soil that remembered footsteps from centuries past, of trees that had witnessed generations come and go like seasons. Yet there was a tenderness and intimacy in the way he sang that transformed the words into something more personal than mere nature poetry.

Georgie leaned forward, caught in the spell of the music. For these few minutes, no one was watching her, analysing her, remembering her failures. All eyes were on Gabe, all thoughts absorbed by the story he was weaving through melody and verse.

As the song reached its bridge, Georgie inclined her head towards Elise.

'Is this about you?' she whispered. The emotion in his voice seemed too intimate, too passionate to be about anything but love.

Elise snorted softly, her eyes never leaving the stage. 'I wish,' she murmured back, a smirk playing at the corners of her mouth. 'It's a love letter to the natural world apparently. Gabe's an eco warrior.'

Georgie clapped a hand over her mouth, shoulders shaking with the effort of containing a laugh. Elise glanced at her, eyebrow raised in mock offence, then her own composure cracked. They leaned together, stifling their giggles like schoolgirls at assembly, though Georgie wouldn't have been at all surprised to discover the song was indeed about Elise, but Gabe didn't want the public to know about it. Maybe one day Elise would walk down the aisle to it and everyone would know the truth of it.

The song reached its emotional peak, Gabe's voice rising as he extolled the virtues of the ancient landscape.

'I'm going to tease him mercilessly about this later,' Elise said as she clapped. 'But don't tell him I said that. I'm very supportive of his artistic vision in public.'

'Let's get some more drinks,' Georgie said.

'My turn.' Elise got up and made her way through the crowd.

Georgie sat alone, pulling out her phone and looking at it only so she looked busy, and not because she actually had anything to look for.

She was so absorbed in faking her interest in her phone she almost missed the conversation floating from the cluster of women nearby. Almost, but not quite.

'—got some nerve, hasn't she? Swanning back like this.'

Georgie's fingers tightened around her phone.

'I mean, she was too big for us then, but now it's all fallen apart, here she is—'

'And didn't she do the dirty on Jake Halley?'

'Yeah. What did happen there?'

'No idea. But I guess he wasn't big enough for her. She went off with that Stefan Varis instead. Though his career tanked too.'

Georgie's face remained perfectly composed, but her skin prickled, and her stomach twisted into a tight knot.

When Elise returned with the drinks, Georgie didn't mention what she'd heard. What was the point? She'd learned over the years she would never be universally popular, but those hateful – and probably alcohol fuelled – words cut deep.

It wasn't really her fault that she'd never come back. Her parents had moved to London to get her the best coaching, and that had become her home in between tour events. And she didn't have to explain that. Still, she couldn't shift a slightly nauseous feeling.

Gabe joined them and sat beside Elise with his arm around her. Georgie didn't mind, but it made her feel out on a limb.

'This is going to be good.' Gabe sipped on a pint as Tavrach took the stage. An electric current seemed to zip through the crowd. The house lights dimmed further, leaving the stage bathed in blue-tinged spotlights that transformed ordinary features into something otherworldly. Four figures moved into position, their instruments like extensions of their bodies rather than separate entities. The pub hushed in anticipation.

The frontman stepped to the microphone, his presence commanding immediate attention. Tall and lean, with dark hair falling past his shoulders, he emanated intensity. Some strands of his hair fell over his face, and he moved his head subtly to clear them. His black vest was well-fitted, and he had inked arms and wrist cuffs.

When he spoke, his voice was a low rumble that somehow carried to every corner of the room without seeming to project. 'Evening, Glenbriar. Let's make some noise.'

The drummer counted them in with four precise taps, and the band launched into their opening number, a driving folk-rock anthem that had the crowd moving within seconds.

The frontman's voice was gravelly and deep, with an emotional rawness that belied the technical control behind it. He could easily be a professional.

Georgie swayed, caught up in the music despite the annoyance of the conversation she'd overheard. Her gaze drifted across the room, and she spotted Kerr, leaning against the wall beside the small tech booth, head nodding in time with the music. Beside him stood Eddie, gesturing animatedly with a pint glass clutched in one hand.

Even in the dim light, Kerr's smile was visible as he listened. He laughed at something Eddie said, then stepped forward to adjust a dial on the soundboard. Georgie gulped some of her cocktail. Kerr might not be the talent on the stage, but he was easily as handsome as any of them. More so.

Tavrach transitioned seamlessly into their second song, this one featuring the guitarist on shared vocals. The contrast was immediately apparent. Where the frontman was all earthy gravitas and raw emotion, this guy had a cleaner, more polished sound. His boyish good looks and carefully styled hair seemed at odds with the band's otherwise rugged aesthetic. He was talented, certainly, but Georgie found herself wondering how the collaboration had come about. They were like different species of the same musical genus – recognisably related but evolved for entirely different environments.

Georgie sipped her drink, eyes drifting back to Kerr. He was focused intently on the sound levels, occasionally making subtle adjustments. As if sensing her attention, he glanced up, eyes scanning the crowd before landing on her.

The moment their gazes connected, something warm unfurled in Georgie's chest. He didn't wave or make any obvious gesture of recognition, just held her eyes for a beat too long to be accidental, the corner of his mouth lifting slightly. Then he turned back to the soundboard, but the brief exchange left Georgie feeling strangely breathless.

At a break in the music, Georgie decided a bathroom trip was an urgent necessity. The floor seemed less stable than it had been earlier, the distance to the ladies' slightly greater, the path considerably more obstacle-strewn.

'Back in a sec,' she told Elise, who was deep in conversation with Gabe, and Hayley, who'd migrated to their table.

The ladies' toilet wasn't too busy, all things considered, and offered a moment of quiet respite from the noise and crush of the main room. She took longer than strictly necessary, splashing cool water on her wrists and checking her reflection in the spotted mirror. Her cheeks were flushed from alcohol and heat, her eyes brighter than usual. She'd only had a couple of drinks, but for someone who rarely touched booze, she was struggling. She reapplied her lip gloss with painstaking attention.

Once she was presentable again, she went into the narrow corridor leading from the toilets to the main room. The hallway opened into a small alcove near the back entrance, where the music – now playing on a recording while the musicians took a break – was slightly muffled. And there, as if conjured by her thoughts, stood Kerr.

He was alone, leaning against the wall, scrolling through something on his phone with a slight frown of concentration. He looked up as she approached, surprise and pleasure replacing the frown in quick succession.

'Georgie.' He pocketed his phone. 'I was just getting some air—'

But Georgie's ankle boot caught on an uneven floorboard, and she stumbled slightly. Kerr's hand shot out reflexively, catching her elbow to steady her.

'Sorry!' she laughed. 'I can't hold my liquor. I barely drank a drop when I was on tour, so a couple of glasses is enough to finish me off.'

His hand remained on her arm. She looked up at him, then placed her own hand on his shoulder.

'Feels like we should dance.'

He raised an eyebrow. 'In the corridor?'

'Why not?'

People were coming and going, but nobody seemed to notice her now, or perhaps the alcohol meant that she wasn't noticing them noticing her... She scrunched up her face, trying to make sense of the thought.

'Because I'm a shit dancer,' Kerr said, but he snaked his arm around her waist and pulled her close. Her breath caught. Why did he make her feel like this? Ways his brother had never managed.

Right now, she couldn't begin to work it out. Her mind was foggy, her insides giddy.

Their eyes held. Their faces were inches apart, close enough that she could feel the warmth of his breath, see the flecks of amber in his hazel eyes. The music continued, but it seemed to fade, as if someone had gradually turned down a dial connecting them to the rest of the world.

Kerr's eyes asked the silent question, 'Do you really want to do this?'

Without hesitation, her lips found his in a clash of heat and hunger.

Georgie gasped into him, breath catching as her back met the wall, his body pressing close, solid and anchoring and utterly overwhelming. The contact sent a shockwave through her, like nerves waking up all at once. His mouth was warm and demanding, coaxing hers open, and when his tongue brushed against hers, a low, involuntary sound escaped her throat. She clutched his shirt, dragging him closer, chasing the kiss like it was oxygen.

And Kerr – God, Kerr – he kissed like a man starved. Every stroke, every shift of his mouth against hers was deep and deliberate. It was molten. He angled his head, deepening the kiss, and the change nearly undid her. Her knees went weak. Her hands fisted the fabric covering his chest, and her whole body lit up with sensation – burning where he touched her, aching where he didn't.

His hand slid from her waist, moving lower, gripping her hip and tugging her closer. Their bodies aligned, chest to chest, heat to heat, and the friction sparked a groan from deep in Kerr's chest that vibrated through her. *Fuck*. This was volcanic. The kind of kiss she'd only ever read about but never experienced for real.

Dizziness overtook her mind; she was drunk on the taste of him – mint and man, the most explosive cocktail she'd tried all evening. His stubble grazed her skin, rough against the softness of her cheek. Every kiss deepened the pull in her belly and tightened the coil of longing low in her spine.

Her fingers skimmed the back of his neck, into his hair, anchoring herself to something real, something she'd craved forever, though she'd never thought it would happen with her ex's brother. Surely that made her all kinds of awful.

He pulled back just enough to breathe, his forehead resting against hers, breaths ragged. His eyes searched hers, stormy and wide, lips red from the kiss, chest rising and falling like he'd just run a sprint.

'Christ, Georgie,' he rasped. 'I've been trying not to do that for years.'

'What?' She gave a shaky laugh, heart pounding like it might never settle. 'Have you?'

He screwed up his face like he'd put his foot in it. 'Yeah. I liked you before Jake asked you out, but I was only fifteen. Part of me still thinks he only did it to annoy me.'

Georgie ran her fingers down his cheek, and an old sensation flickered in her chest. 'I see.' Things made more sense now, especially after hearing that Kerr's family worried about Jake's mental health but couldn't get him to seek help. Jake wasn't a bad guy, but he was clingy. And Georgie had always had a sense that his desperation had other motives. Perhaps wanting to have something to hold over the younger brother, who was altogether cheerier and more popular, had been an underlying motivation – whether conscious or not.

'Sorry. I killed the mood.' Kerr raked his fingers through his hair.

'No, you didn't. You've just cleared something up in my mind.'

'Oh yeah? What's that? That you don't want anything to do with me?'

'No... That I want you to kiss me again.'

His mouth was on hers faster than a first serve, and deeper this time – like the first had just been the warmup and this was the championship match. And there was so much at stake. So much that hinged on this moment.

Chapter Eighteen

Kerr

Georgie's lips were soft but insistent; her fingers tugged Kerr's hair, just enough to short-circuit his thoughts. He pressed her harder into the wall, his thigh slipping between hers, and her breath hitched against his mouth. Christ. Her hips shifted, meeting his like a challenge, and the friction lit up every nerve ending he had.

This wasn't a kiss. It was a full-body blackout.

His hands found her waist, skimming under the hem of her silky top. Warm skin met his palms, and she arched into him. The brush of lace beneath his fingers almost fried his brain.

'Christ, Georgie,' he murmured into her neck, where he'd moved to press a line of open-mouthed kisses against her jaw. 'You're—' He didn't even know what the end of that sentence was meant to be. Gorgeous. Perfect. Dangerous.

She let out a breathy sound and dragged his mouth back to hers. Her kiss was all tongue and teeth and fire, leaving no room for thinking. Only doing. Desiring.

His body was fully up for the task. Unfortunately, the timing was shit. Somewhere in the depths of his kiss-drugged mind, he registered the faint shift in music – the opening beat of a drum check, maybe. Sound bled from the main room.

He groaned, resting his forehead against hers. 'We need to stop.'

'Please don't,' she said, breathless, chasing his lips.

He kissed her again because he couldn't not – a hard, hot clash that made his self-control hang by a thread. Then he pulled back, just enough.

'Break's nearly over. If I don't get back in there, I'll be in trouble.'

Georgie narrowed her eyes like she might argue, but she was panting too, flushed, wild and gorgeous.

He gave her waist a final squeeze, then stepped back, hand dragging slowly from her skin like he couldn't quite let go.

'Sorry.' He raised his shoulder slightly. 'But I really have to get back in there.'

She nodded, licking her lips, clearly trying to get herself together. 'Yeah. Of course.'

He turned, adjusted himself as discreetly as possible, and headed for the door.

The crowd had thickened by the time Kerr pushed back into the main room. Bodies jostled, drinks sloshed, laughter bounced off the low ceiling. Someone bumped into him and muttered an apology over the bass thrum starting up again.

He slid behind the sound desk, flicked a few faders, and nodded at the band. Tavrach were already tuning up – Adam strumming absently, Ailsa twirling a stick between her fingers.

Kerr's fingers moved on autopilot. Volume levels. EQ. Reverb tweaks. None of this should be a problem.

But his head was a fucking mess.

Georgie's kiss burned on his lips, like it had left an imprint. Her taste. The feel of her body pressed to his. That breathy sound she'd made when he'd backed her against the wall—

He swore under his breath and forced himself to focus.

Adam launched into the first track, and Kerr adjusted the mix, checking the balance between guitar and vocal.

Where was she?

His gaze scanned the room, barely registering the faces he passed. A sea of punters, but no Georgie.

The song changed. He barely noticed. Tavrach played on, and he made the adjustments they needed, forcing his brain to focus. Letting thoughts of Georgie take over now was ridiculous. Because he loved music and this event. Being part of it was supposed to be exciting and fun. But all he could think about was *her*.

All the years of tension and dreaming had been whipped away. One kiss – ok, one world-ending, brain-melting kiss – and it felt like something had cracked open inside him.

Not the time. Not the place.

And definitely not the headspace for it, not with bass feedback threatening and the next singer waiting on deck. Kerr leaned in, flicked a switch, gestured to the guy with the acoustic guitar to get ready. He caught the beat drop and patched in the next mic.

Still no sign of her.

His eyes kept drifting, skimming around. But the pub was dark, the lights were low, and the air was thick with noise.

No space to think.

No clarity.

Just the ghost of her kiss, and the crash of drums ringing in his ears.

When the last chord rang out to cheers and a few overenthusiastic whoops, Kerr dipped the levels, killed the stage mics and flicked the desk to standby. Tavrach waved their thanks and started packing down, the room still buzzing with post-gig energy.

Kerr exhaled, hands finally still. His neck ached from craning round the desk, and his back had a tight pull across one shoulder, but it was background noise compared to the hum running through him.

He coiled cables, wound them tight, tucked them under the desk. A few punters filtered out. Others queued at the bar, trying to squeeze one last round before closing. The lights had come up a fraction – not full glare, but enough to strip the magic from the corners.

Still no sign of Georgie.

He shoved the last lead into the flight case and clicked it shut, wiping his palms on his jeans. He was sweating, though the room had cooled. Not just from the work. His skin still prickled with the phantom feel of her hands. He craved more of that. Much more.

'Here we go.' Eddie appeared beside him, holding out a pint with a crooked grin. 'For services to excellent sound quality.'

Kerr took the pint, cool condensation slick against his fingers.

'Cheers,' he muttered, taking a long pull. It hit the back of his throat sharp and cold.

Eddie leaned on the edge of the desk, watching him. 'You ok?'

'Yeah, fine. That was tiring, that's all.'

'Yes, you look a bit spaced.'

Kerr pulled out his phone and checked it. 'Fuck's sake.'

He saw a message from Jake. No way could his brother know what had happened between Kerr and Georgie just an hour ago, but it felt weirdly like he did and this was his warning arriving. That said, this pub was packed with locals. Anyone could have seen them in the corridor. But would they report back to Jake?

'Problem?' Eddie peered at him.

'A message from Jake.' He placed his pint down and opened his screen. The only way he would find out what Jake knew... or didn't. Was to actually read the message.

JAKE: Loads to tell you. All shit really. Genna's been cheating on me.

Kerr's eyes widened, and he ran his fingers through his hair. Jake and Genna had been engaged and were planning a wedding.

And if that's not enough, the flat's in her name. She wants me out by the end of the week. Says she "needs space" to "figure things out". So fuck knows what I'm going to do. Just to keep you up to speed on where my shitshow of a life is at. Ever since Georgie turned up at your door, I've had a bad feeling. It's like she's jinxed my whole life.

Guilt twisted in Kerr's stomach like a live thing. Just a couple of hours ago, he'd had his hands in Georgie Porter's hair, his lips on hers, his body pressed against the woman who'd broken his brother's heart – or at least sent him spiralling. And Kerr didn't want that on his conscience. For all Jake had his issues, he'd been there for Kerr after the Anna breakup. Kerr had spent a summer in London with him, and he'd been great. But Jake had so many ups and downs. And if he and Genna had split, he wouldn't need much more to tip him over the edge.

'I need some air.' Kerr pocketed his phone and lifted his pint.

'On your own?' Eddie raised his eyebrows, concern etched into the lines on his brow. 'Or is it something you want to talk about?'

'Yeah, come with me.'

The night air hit Kerr like a slap, cool and clarifying after the stuffy heat of the Stagger Inn. He leaned against the rough stone wall, tilting his head back.

Eddie put his hand on Kerr's shoulder. 'What's happened?'

Kerr explained Jake's message.

'Hmm.' Eddie let out a little sigh. 'I feel sorry for him, but why is it making you feel so bad? You're not responsible.'

'Maybe not... But...' He glanced at the door. 'Things have got heated between Georgie and me.'

'Meaning what exactly?'

'We... kissed. Just now. During the break.'

'Ok.' Eddie nodded, his expression kind. 'For any particular reason?'

Kerr stared into his glass. 'Because I've fancied her for years. I liked her before Jake did. When I was too young. All the time I had to be gutted for him when he split up with her, I was just as gutted for myself because I knew I'd never have a chance. And just there... That was a chance, and I took it. But of course I shouldn't have. All I've done is betray my brother.'

Eddie nodded slowly. 'The eternal burden of the loyal brother.' He took a sip of his own drink. 'Really, Kerr. It shouldn't be up to your brother to dictate who you kiss.'

'I know, but it makes everything awkward. Like every time I talk to him, I'm lying.'

'Which you are. You've lied about your feelings for Georgie forever, it seems. When you say you liked her before he dated her, I assume he didn't know how you felt.'

'He did. I told him. But I was only fifteen. He asked her out and didn't give me a chance to air my feelings. And he was pissed at me for getting on the school tennis team when he didn't. He just said something like, "You liked her a bit for a while too, didn't you? But she's too old for you anyway".'

'Oh dear.' Eddie shook his head. 'Loyalty is a fine quality. One of the finest. But there's a difference between loyalty and self-subjugation. And you realise what Jake did in the first place was very cruel.'

'But there's more. I think he's depressed, or…' Kerr held out his hands '…there's something troubling him mentally and emotionally. But he won't get help. And he hates people even mentioning it.'

'That puts you in a very difficult position. I can see that.' Eddie finished his pint. 'Thing is, Kerr, nothing erases the past, but must it dictate the future? Must Jake's hurt feelings from years ago determine your choices now?'

Kerr took another drink. There was wisdom there, but also a simplicity that didn't account for the complex family web and shared history.

'You make it sound so easy. Just choose my own happiness, Jake's feelings be damned.'

Eddie chuckled. 'Nothing about relationships is ever straightforward. You already know that after what you went through with your last girlfriend. Sometimes, doing right by yourself is the bravest choice you can make.'

Eddie rarely spoke of his early days of coming out, but Kerr knew it hadn't been easy.

'I don't want to send him into another pit of despair,' Kerr said quietly.

'Of course you don't.' Eddie tightened his grip on Kerr's shoulder. 'But it seems to me that he quite likes being there. He feeds off this kind of negativity. It's not healthy, but it gets him attention. I get the feeling that he wouldn't necessarily be angry with you for seeing Georgie, just that he would relish the chance to be angry about something. Do you see what I'm saying?'

'Yes. And you're probably right. So... do you think I should see Georgie? I mean... what if I get attached to her and then she leaves? Just like Anna did?'

'Well.' Eddie flapped a hand in front of his face to stifle a yawn. 'Sorry, it's late and I'm tired out, but I don't think you should compare Georgie to Anna. Let the situation with Georgie play out and see where it takes you. Believe me, regret is worse than not acting.' He checked his phone. 'I need to go home to bed. I'll call Kenneth to come for me. You should go home too. Sleep on it.' He fired away a quick text. 'I'll nip to the bathroom first. If I don't see you before I go, bye-bye. I'll message you tomorrow.'

Kerr gave him a brief hug. 'Thanks, mate. I appreciate it.'

Eddie clapped his back and headed back inside on his phone.

Kerr went to return his glass before he left, but people were spilling out of the door, and he stepped back to let them leave.

As he waited, his eyes landed on one of them, and his heart stopped momentarily.

Georgie stepped fully outside, whispering something to Elise, then stepping to the side, closer to Kerr.

'Hey,' she said. 'I thought you'd left.'

'Same. I didn't see you in there.'

'We were squashed at the back... Listen, I, um, can we talk?'

'Sure.' Did she want to apologise? Maybe he should. No doubt this was where she told him she regretted what they'd just done. 'About that kiss?' He gave a nonchalant shrug.

'No... not that. I actually wanted to ask you something.' Her fingers played with the zip of her rust-coloured jacket. 'I was going to ask you the other day at the tennis club, but I didn't have the chance. I'm not sure if this is something you'll want to do... but, um, would you like to come to Hayley's wedding with me? As my plus-one.'

Kerr blinked, caught off guard by this glimpse of a parallel reality – one where Jake's message and the history Georgie had with him were inconsequential. One where the kiss could exist as a prelude to something more.

'Hayley's wedding...' he repeated.

'It's next weekend.' A rueful smile tugged at the corner of her mouth. 'Short notice, I know.' She shrugged. 'And I know it's probably not sensible, but we... well, we seem to get on pretty well. It was just a thought. Silly, really.'

'Not silly.' Kerr gently took hold of her arm as she seemed on the verge of walking away. 'Not silly at all.'

Georgie studied his face, her gaze searching. 'So, you want to?'

'Yeah... I do. I mean, it could cause problems, but you know what? I want to spend time with you. This might be stupid, but I feel like I've been robbed and I want to make up for lost time.'

'Aw.' She smiled and took his hand. 'And I'd like to spend more time with you. You're a fun guy.'

'What like the mushrooms?' He snorted.

She play-slapped his arm. 'Yeah, just like them... Listen, how about we start right now?'

'Start what?'

'Spending some time together.'

The night air was cool around them, but her hand in his was warm – and for once, that warmth didn't feel like something he had to let go. 'Ok. Sure.'

Chapter Nineteen

Georgie

Georgie held tight to Kerr's hand. It didn't seem like he would let go, but she didn't want to take the chance. The crowd had moved away from the door of The Stagger Inn, and the street was quieter now. A few drops of rain touched Georgie's skin as she waited for Kerr to reply.

When she'd suggested they start spending time together right now, she wasn't entirely sure exactly what she meant. The alcohol was partly to blame, but so was her uncertainty about her feelings for Kerr and the complications that came with acknowledging the truth of them.

'How are you getting back to Heather Glen?' he asked.

'I'm not going back tonight. I brought the van here, and I parked her on a side street. Probably illegal, but hopefully no one will notice.'

Kerr smirked. 'I don't think it's illegal, is it? Only in car parks where it specifically says no overnight camping. And even then, I've seen lots of people who do.'

'Well, then... that's fine. Do you want to join me?'

He raised an eyebrow, then looked away and ran his free hand through his hair. 'No, I don't think so.'

Georgie's insides slumped. 'Oh, ok.'

'I'd rather sleep in my own bed tonight.' He glanced back at her. 'But I wouldn't mind if you were in it with me.'

The laugh that escaped her was almost pure relief, though within a second, prickles of excitement were tickling her, and her giggling became almost uncontrollable.

'Though I'm not sure you're fit for anything too... strenuous.' Kerr eyed her over. 'How drunk are you?'

'Honestly, I've only had two drinks. I'm fine. Just emotional. My life recently has been so weird, and now standing out on a damp street discussing sleeping with you in such a matter-of-fact way is just so... I don't know. Bizarre.'

'Let's walk.' He tugged her hand. 'The fresh air will help.'

'With what?'

'To clear our heads.'

'Is that a fact or just you hoping?'

'A bit of both, I think.'

They walked along the main street, rain falling gently enough to be more a pleasure than a nuisance.

'The Stagger Inn always had a reputation for being the noisiest place in town, didn't it?' Georgie glanced back at it. 'Everywhere else seems a bit too quiet now.'

Kerr increased the pressure on her hand a little. 'Maybe you should sing, or something... Make some noise of your own.'

'I'm a terrible singer.'

Kerr laughed, and somehow it transformed into a snatch of song – just a few notes, deep, and somewhat gobbledygook, but clearly an attempt at one of Tavrach's songs.

'They're really good,' she said, 'though I didn't catch all the lyrics. Do they write them all themselves?'

'As far as I know.' He continued, making up nonsensical lyrics about rain and autumn colours to fit in with the tune.

Georgie's giggles returned, and she joined in the song, contributing more silly rhymes, until they were both half-singing, half-laughing their way up the empty street towards Kirk Lane. The cobbled road was dappled with fallen leaves that squished beneath their feet. Streetlamps cast golden halos on the wet tarmac, making puddles shimmer like little pools of firelight.

In what seemed like no time at all, they were back at Kerr's house. He unlocked the door, and they stepped inside.

Georgie slipped off her jacket, suddenly conscious of being in his space again. And to be honest, completely out of her depth. She'd never really hooked up or dated in a normal way. What was the etiquette? The rules? Christ, she hadn't even considered the practicalities. She was on birth control – mostly to regulate her cycle for when she'd been on tour. It had made tournament preparation easier to know exactly when her period would arrive. But what about safety? She definitely didn't carry condoms.

'Let me.' Kerr reached for her damp jacket and helped her take it off. He hung it on a hook in the corridor, smiling at her, then he raised his hand to her hair and combed his fingers through it gently. 'I've wanted to do this for a long time,' he said. 'But is it weird for you? Because... Well, I guess you and Jake...'

She shook her head. 'We never got further than kissing.' And even that had been stilted. 'Something always happened.' Maybe that something had been her. She couldn't escape the sense that she'd never really wanted to be with Jake. But here and now with Kerr, that was a different story.

'I see.' He let out a sigh. 'I wish...'

'What?'

'That he'd never asked you out in the first place.'

Georgie bit her lip. 'And I wish I'd never said yes. I think I only did it because everyone was dating someone... And well, I kind of felt sorry for him. He wanted to get on the tennis team, and he said he'd like to practise with me.'

Kerr frowned. 'Sounds about right. I was on the team, and he was annoyed that he didn't get picked. I always suspected that had something to do with it.'

'Well, you were right. I didn't expect the relationship with Jake to carry on once I left Glenbriar. If I'd just had the guts to call it off. Instead... Well, it all got messy, as you know.'

'Do you remember his graduation?'

She nodded.

'And we had that moment? Or was that just my imagination?'

She shook her head. 'I felt it too. It was the weirdest thing. Like I felt more for you in those few seconds than I did in all the years with Jake. It hit me so hard. I left after that, and it was the springboard for me accepting the relationship with Stefan.'

'Really?'

'Yeah. I guess it made me realise I wasn't really attracted to Jake. But I didn't know how to tell him without upsetting him. The way he clung on every time I tried. It wasn't healthy, but I was young, inexperienced, and totally clueless. I see that now.'

'I was so angry with him for asking you out in the first place.'

'Did you say anything to him?'

'I did, but… Well, just like you, I didn't want to upset him. And I respected your choice.'

She let out a sigh. 'I made a mistake. I'd wanted to break up with Jake when I left Glenbriar, but I'll never stop feeling guilty about the way it actually happened.'

'Be free of it,' Kerr said firmly. 'Let's put it in the past. You offered an apology to Jake, and he didn't want to accept it. As for us.' His eyes bored into hers.

She smiled. 'Can we start with a clean sheet?'

'Let's try. Because if Jake had been as loyal to me as I've been to him over the years, he would never have asked you in the first place.'

'What a mess.' She lowered her head, staring at her feet.

Kerr's hands slipped around her face. 'Maybe, but life is like that.' He captured her lips. His thumb traced the line of her cheekbone. Georgie leaned into him, her hands finding the solid warmth of his chest.

She let out a soft moan as Kerr pulled her flush against him and gasped against his mouth at the sudden closeness; the heat of him seeped through the thin fabric of her camisole.

They stumbled backwards in the narrow hallway. Kerr's back hit the wall with a soft thud, and Georgie pressed her advantage, rising onto her toes to better access his mouth. His hands slid lower, spanning her waist and then settling at her hips, fingers digging in just enough to send sparks racing along her nerve endings.

'Too good,' he breathed against her lips.

She slid her fingers into his hair, angling his head to deepen the kiss. The taste of him was intoxicating, more potent than the cocktails. He skimmed the hem of her black camisole.

'Can I?' he whispered.

'Yes.' She lifted her arms to assist. 'But I need to tell you... I don't carry condoms, and I don't want to do anything silly.'

'That's ok.' He drew the camisole over her head, the movement revealing her black lace bra beneath. His breath audibly caught as he took her in, the raw appreciation in his expression making her feel more beautiful than any photographer's lens ever had. 'I have everything we need, and we don't have to do anything you don't want to.'

'I want to be with you.'

Kerr tugged off his T-shirt in one fluid motion, revealing his defined chest. A light dusting of brown hair narrowed as it disappeared beneath his jeans, drawing her eye downward. Unlike when they were in the van, this time, she was allowed to look. Allowed to touch.

They crashed together again, the contact of skin against skin electrifying. Georgie ran her hands over the planes of his back, pulling him close while his mouth explored the delicate curve where her neck met her shoulder. The scratch of his evening stubble against her skin sent shivers cascading down her spine, pooling low in her belly.

His fingers edged to the clasp of her bra, hesitating until she nodded her permission. He unhooked it, sliding the straps down her arms until the garment fell away completely. The warmth of his palms immediately replaced the cool air against her exposed breasts.

'Oh god,' she groaned, arching into him.

'You're so beautiful,' he murmured.

Georgie started working on his jeans, need making her fingers clumsy. Kerr helped her, and she pushed both jeans and boxers down his hips impatiently. She was rewarded with his sharp intake of breath as her fingers grazed over him.

He popped the button of her high-waisted jeans, sliding the zip down. As the denim parted, he dipped his head to trail kisses along her collarbone, dropping lower until his mouth found her breast.

'I think we should move this upstairs,' Kerr managed between kisses.

'Uh-huh.' Georgie kicked off her heeled boots as Kerr stepped out of his own footwear, both of them fumbling with socks and laughing.

'So smooth,' Kerr muttered.

'Who cares?' She followed him up the narrow, steep stairs. 'It's not like anyone is watching.'

Georgie had shared her body before, but rarely herself. Being this unguarded, laughing at how unsophisticated they must look, and feeling no pressure to be perfect was so freeing and new.

As they settled onto Kerr's bed, the sheets felt cool beneath her, but he was like a furnace next to her. They lay facing each other, and she reached for him, palm flat against his chest where she felt the strong, steady rhythm of his heart. He mirrored her gesture, his hand spanning her waist, thumb gently stroking her hipbone.

They fell into a long, deep kiss. Kerr made a sound low in his throat as his arm wrapped around her, drawing her flush against him.

The full-body contact sent a cascade of sensation through Georgie, the press of his chest against her breasts, the hardness of his arousal against her thigh, the scratch of his stubble against her smoother skin. It was overwhelming in the best possible way.

'You're incredible,' he murmured.

Before she could respond, his mouth closed over one nipple, tongue circling the sensitive peak. A soft moan escaped her. Her fingers threaded through his soft hair, holding him to her as pleasure spiralled outward from the point of contact. His hand attended to her other breast, thumb and forefinger working together with his mouth.

She relinquished conscious thought and gave herself over to indulging the sensations.

Her hand drifted downward, tracing the line of muscle that disappeared beneath his navel before moving lower. Kerr inhaled sharply as she encircled him, his forehead pressing against her collarbone.

'Is this good?' she whispered.

'Perfect.' The word was a half-groan against her skin. 'You're perfect.'

He glided his palm from her breast, ever lower until he reached her inner thigh. Each pass brought his fingers closer to where she ached for him, the anticipation almost as intoxicating as the contact itself. When he finally touched her, she threw her head back and moaned.

Her hand on him faltered as pleasure overtook her ability to concentrate.

'Don't stop,' she gasped, hips rocking against his hand. 'Please don't stop.'

'I won't,' he said.

And she trusted him not to. Not until she'd hit the climax she wanted so badly. It had been a long time, and fires were quickly igniting inside her.

Kerr's mouth found hers again, swallowing her increasingly vocal responses as he drove her higher.

And then a tsunami swept her under, obliterating thought and reason. She cried out against his mouth, body arcing and trembling as pleasure radiated in electric pulses. Kerr held her through it, drawing out every aftershock until she collapsed back against the pillows, breathless and dazed.

As reality slowly reassembled itself, Georgie noticed Kerr watching her, as if he'd witnessed something miraculous. And maybe he had. This wasn't exactly an everyday occurrence.

For a few moments, they were almost still, just holding each other, gently moving their hands, but Georgie didn't want it to end here.

'We're not done,' she told him. 'Not even close.'

'Good.' He moved on top of her, kissing along her shoulder. 'Because I have lots more for you.'

He kneeled up and reached towards the side of the bed. 'Ok, give me a minute,' he said. 'You can enjoy more of my smooth moves.'

Georgie bit back a smile as he leaned over the edge of the bed, fishing beneath the bed frame. He sat up with a small box, extracting a foil packet.

'It might have been sensible to get this out first, but hey.' He shrugged and rolled the condom.

'It all adds to the experience.' Georgie giggled. 'Keeps it real.'

'Oh, it's real alright.' Kerr placed his hands on either side of her hips and tugged her towards him. She parted her legs to welcome him.

Their bodies aligned, and with deliberate slowness, he pressed forward. The initial sensation of him entering her drew a gasp from her lips, her body stretching to accommodate him in a pleasure so acute it bordered on discomfort.

'All ok?' he whispered.

'More than.' She lifted her hips to take him deeper. They stayed like that for a moment – joined completely, adjusting to the overwhelming intimacy of being so connected. Tears pricked unexpectedly at the corners of her eyes, not from pain but from the sheer intensity of the moment, the vulnerability of being so utterly open to another person.

Kerr began to move, setting a gentle rhythm that quickly built as their bodies found synchronicity. Each thrust sent waves of pleasure radiating through Georgie, building upon the lingering sensitivity. She wrapped her legs around his waist, changing the angle slightly and drawing a shuddered breath from them both as he pressed deeper.

'You're amazing,' he murmured against her neck, pulling her closer. 'So perfect.'

The warm, gentle lovingness of him, alongside the raw heat, was almost unbearable. This would break her – emotionally. She moved with him, meeting each thrust, hands mapping the contours of his back, his shoulders. The steady friction against her most sensitive parts combined with the deeper penetration that touched a secret place within her, building a different kind of tension than before, fuller, deeper, more all-encompassing.

'Oh Georgie,' he groaned. 'I've wanted this for so long.'

The sound of her name on his lips brought a rising wave that lifted her higher and higher until she crested with a cry. Her body clenched around him, surges of pleasure pulsing through her.

His movements grew more urgent, chasing his own release even as he prolonged hers. Georgie, still riding the aftershocks of her pleasure, urged him on, hands pulling him deeper, wanting to witness his abandon.

When it came, it transformed him – all the careful control gave way to something primal and beautiful. His body tensed, a sound escaping him that was half-groan, half-her name. Georgie held him through it. Time seemed suspended for a moment, and they stayed still, except for the rise and fall of their chests.

Slowly they moved into a more comfortable position, though still tangled together. Kerr pressed a gentle kiss to her temple. 'I'm not sure that was my best effort. I was too desperate.'

She chuckled. 'It seemed pretty good to me... Though maybe the next time, you can show me some more of your impressive moves.'

He didn't reply but kissed her again. Maybe there wouldn't be a next time. Georgie had no idea where this might go. For now, though, she had this, and it was enough.

Whatever complications tomorrow might bring was something she wasn't going to worry about until daylight arrived. Right now, she was simply going to enjoy the sense that she belonged here, and, for this moment, she was in the perfect place.

Chapter Twenty

Kerr

For a suspended moment, Kerr's sleep-fogged brain couldn't place the unfamiliar weight across his chest and the scent of someone else's shampoo on his pillow – then memory rushed back. He kept his eyes closed.

Georgie's arm lay draped across his chest, her breathing deep and even against his side, hair spilled across his shoulder in a tangle of brown.

Carefully, trying not to disturb her, Kerr shifted just enough to see her face. She'd hardly changed in all the years he'd known her, the light tan, the freckles, the long dark hair. Or maybe it was just because he'd seen her so often on TV that she seemed so familiar.

She stirred against him, eyelashes fluttering, and he twitched slightly, then held his breath. Morning-afters had rules, didn't they? Though he wasn't sure he knew what they were. He hadn't hooked up in a long time. Not since his breakup. He'd considered online dating and once even considered going out with someone his mum knew, but neither had actually happened.

'Hi,' she murmured.

'Hi. How did you sleep?'

'Good.' She stretched slightly, catlike, against him. 'Better than I normally do in the van. You?'

'Same.' He traced a finger along the soft skin of her arm. 'Though I'm still not entirely convinced last night wasn't a dream.'

Her smile widened. 'Want me to pinch you?'

'I can think of better ways to confirm reality.'

Georgie laughed, then grimaced slightly. 'Sorry, morning breath.'

'No worries. I need to pee.' Kerr reluctantly detached himself from her warmth, sliding out of bed. 'Give me two minutes.'

In his small bathroom, he caught sight of himself in the mirror – hair standing in every direction, and stubble darkening his jaw.

He went for a pee, brushed his teeth quickly, then retrieved a new toothbrush from the cabinet and a small bottle of mouthwash. When he returned to the bedroom, Georgie had pulled the sheet up over her chest, but her bare shoulders and the messy sprawl of her hair against his pillows sent a pulse of desire through him that surprised him with its intensity.

'I left you a spare toothbrush in the bathroom, if you want it. Not that you smell bad or anything, but because you mentioned it.'

'Aw, you're sweet.' She got up and disappeared into the bathroom.

Kerr heard the water running, pictured her bent over his sink, using his things, and felt a strange domestic pleasure at the thought. He straightened the duvet and got back into the bed.

When she returned, she got back into the bed with him, ran her hand around his jaw and pulled him in for a kiss.

'No rushing this time,' he murmured.

'We have all morning,' she said. 'I'm teaching some kids at the tennis club later, but not until two.'

'Are you?' This was new. Did it mean she was seriously considering putting down roots?

'Amanda asked me to do some coaching with her daughter and some of her friends. I said yes. It's not like I'm doing anything else... Well, apart from this.'

He smiled and pushed her gently on to her back. 'Then let's have some fun.'

They kissed deeply, just existing in its decadence. Their hands moved, finding all the right places, both letting out soft moans and sighs.

There was no alcohol or urgency this time, just desire and the luxury of time. Kerr rolled them until she lay beneath him, her hair spread across his pillow like spilled ink. He kissed her all over, placing kisses on her sensitive skin and most intimate places, until she was a writhing, squirming and joyful mess.

When he knew she was sated with pleasure, he put on another condom, and they made love slowly, taking time to look at each other, smile, and kiss.

She moved on top of him, straddling him and establishing a rhythm that was clearly enhancing her pleasure. He fixed his hands on her hips, meeting her movements. Then she lowered her head to kiss him as they moved together, and their bodies were like one being. A being with the sole purpose of creating bliss.

Her hands clutched at his shoulders, nails digging into him. The slight pain only heightened his awareness of her pleasure, and the way her body tightened around him. When she began to tremble, he slipped a hand between them, finding the sensitive bundle of nerves that would push her over the edge.

'Yes,' she gasped against his mouth, 'there, just like—'

She broke apart, slumping onto him, her body clenching in rhythmic pulses that tested his control to its limits. He slowed his movements, letting her ride out the waves of pleasure, watching in awe as her face transformed with it – all guard down, all pretence gone, just pure unfiltered sensation.

'That really was so good.' Still panting, she nuzzled into his shoulder. 'I'm just happy in your company. I don't feel like I have to put on a show.'

'You don't. Just be you. The real you.' His words were breathy. He began to move again, deeper, more purposeful, each thrust a promise. Georgie responded immediately, her body slamming down to meet his. 'I want you...' he groaned as the pressure built. 'I want you as you are now.' The past didn't even matter. He hadn't known her properly back then. What he liked was who she'd become.

Consequences be damned.

For now anyway.

'You've got me,' she whispered in his ear. 'And it's you I want.'

'Oh god.' Pleasure raged through him, more intense than anything he'd experienced before. She was his. And he was hers. The world was the most amazing place.

He gathered her against him as their breathing gradually slowed, and their heartbeats found a shared rhythm.

Kerr pressed his lips to her temple. How easy would it be to shut out the world and just exist like this forever?

Easy maybe. But not practical.

'How about we shower and have breakfast?' he suggested.

'When you say "we" shower... do you mean together?'

'Sure.' He glanced down at her, and her eyelids fluttered at him. 'I've never shared a shower with anyone before, but I'm happy to change that.'

'I've shared communal showers at tournaments occasionally, but that's not the kind of shower you have in mind, is it?'

'Definitely not... This one will be a lot hotter.'

Steam curled in the air, thick and fragrant with citrus and tea tree. The bathroom tiles gleamed under the slow trickle of water.

It could have been awkward, but it wasn't. Not with Georgie. Nothing about her felt like too much. In fact, it was the opposite. Every breath she took, every pass of her fingers over his shoulders or scrape of nails down his back, only made him want more. Her wet skin against his, slick with soap and heat, was enough to scramble his thoughts and tighten every muscle in his body.

She laughed – low and wicked – when his hands found her hips, and the sound shot straight through him, more powerful than anything he'd heard onstage.

There was kissing. God, there was kissing. Deep, wet, lazy kisses that turned hungry, then soft again. He sucked water droplets from her full lips.

Time slipped, and even when the water cooled a little, he couldn't bring himself to stop touching her. He turned her to face the tiles, so her back was to him and her body fit against his so perfectly, like it was meant to be nowhere else, but pressed to him in the mist. He wrapped his arms around her, smoothing his palms over her breasts, stomach, and lower, as he sheathed himself, and filled her again. They both moaned and panted, moving together, grunting as they took their fill of each other.

Eventually, they stumbled out, flushed and dripping, wrapped in towels and each other's arms.

Kerr had never started a day like this before. And he already knew he'd never forget it.

'I need to go back to the van and get dressed properly,' Georgie said, as Kerr made them some scrambled eggs flecked with red pepper. 'I can't go to the courts dressed like this.'

She'd put on her clothes from last night.

'Which side street are you parked on?'

'The Back Wynd.'

'That's not too far.' Kerr put a plate in front of her. 'It's just five minutes away.'

'Yeah.' She smiled at him. 'Thanks.'

'What for?'

'Breakfast... And...' She lifted her right shoulder. 'For spending time with me.'

'Happy to.' He took a mouthful of scrambled eggs.

'And you're still ok to come to Hayley's wedding with me?'

He chewed his mouthful slowly. 'Yeah, sure. Thankfully, I don't think too many people in the town know about what happened with you and Jake, so it should be safe enough.'

'I hope so.' She maintained eye contact. 'I don't regret what we did. I know things are complicated with Jake, but I don't think we should let that ruin how we feel now.'

'Let's just take things slowly.' Because there was no certainty that she would stick around long enough for this to be anything more than a short fling.

Before she left, he kissed her goodbye. At least if they were going to the wedding together, they had a concrete date to see each other again.

The house felt weirdly empty without her. Weird, because he was used to being alone here on Sundays, but not lonely. He half wished he'd gone to the courts with her just to knock about. There was work he could do, but this was the start of half term and he'd really rather not.

In the kitchen, he washed their breakfast dishes and put them away. Mundane tasks were a good way to keep busy.

He'd just finished tidying when his phone buzzed. If it was Eddie, he would be overjoyed. Who else would listen so well when he wanted to pour out his soul?

But his mum's name flashed on the screen, accompanied by the photo she'd insisted on taking last Christmas of the whole family in silly jumpers.

'Hi, Mum,' he answered, cradling the phone between ear and shoulder as he dried his hands on a tea towel. Had things been different, he would've liked to be able to confide in his parents, but how would that work in this instance? He couldn't make them choose between sons... And although maybe that wasn't exactly what was happening, it seemed they were on the edge of a battle he'd tried to avoid for years.

'Kerr, darling. How was the festival opening night?'

'Really good. It went well.'

'Aw, I'm glad.' In the background, Kerr heard what sounded like cupboard doors opening and closing. 'Listen, did Jake message you about the split with his girlfriend?'

'Yeah, he did.' Kerr rubbed the back of his neck.

'What a mess. Poor Jake. Anyway, the good news is, it means he's coming home.'

'What?' Kerr swallowed.

'Well, he can do his job from anywhere really, and I think he needs to get himself away from the situation. So, he's agreed to come back. He's going to stay with us for a while until he sorts himself out.'

The pressure in the room seemed to compress, making it harder to breathe.

'That's... great,' Kerr managed. 'It'll be good to see him.'

Jesus Christ.

How was this going to work? Getting together with Georgie while Jake was in London was one thing, but if he was here...

Kerr buried his face in his hands.

Why was this happening? Why had he gone and fallen so hard for Georgie?

Eddie had made it sound easy – choose your own happiness, live your own life, trust yourself. Was it that simple?

The new feelings he was nurturing for Georgie couldn't remain hidden from Jake forever – not if Kerr was to choose Georgie as he really wanted to. That day of reckoning was coming, and he wasn't sure if he was ready to face it.

Chapter Twenty-One

Georgie

The curved ceiling of the campervan closed in on Georgie as she attempted to zip up her emerald satin dress, elbows knocking against the compact wardrobe for the third time. What had once felt like cosy freedom now seemed like a ridiculous challenge, and one she was losing patience with. She twisted awkwardly, fingers straining for the zip that remained stubbornly out of reach. One month ago, living in the van had felt like an adventure, a declaration of independence. Now she'd had enough.

'For god's sake,' she muttered, finally yanking up the zip. Her original mission had taken such a detour. Mostly a pleasant one. Well, she liked spending time with Kerr, with her friends, working on the coaching and the MUGA, and just being in Glenbriar. But if that was going to continue, she needed to find somewhere more permanent than the van, especially now that October had arrived.

She sank onto the edge of her bed-slash-seating-area, smoothing down the satin of the dress she'd bought in a local boutique to wear to Hayley's wedding. Her parents were pressuring her to come home, and even her former agent had been in touch, saying he'd heard of some new opportunities for her and would be happy to work with her again if she wanted to explore any of them.

She wasn't sure she wanted to, but maybe she should.

With Kerr being on half term, she'd seen him more in the past week when he wasn't doing things at the music festival. But the day after they first got together, he'd dropped a bomb... Jake was back. And not just back. He was already in a bad place. His proximity had brought a downer to every meeting she and Kerr had. Even now, the tension gripped her shoulders the same way it had done before a big match. Only this time, she didn't feel confident about meeting the opponent.

She got into the driver's seat and headed into Glenbriar. It was Friday night and lots of party-goers hung around outside the Stagger Inn. Georgie had arranged to pick up Kerr from his house, then drive to the wedding venue – a big country house named Thistle Lodge where they would join the evening reception of Hayley's wedding.

Apparently, Thistle Lodge had a large private car park, so Georgie planned to leave the van there. That way, she and Kerr could have a drink, spend the night in the van, then return the next day.

When she arrived at his house, he waved from inside the door, then came out and locked it before jumping into the van. He wore a perfectly fitted navy suit with a crisp white shirt open at the collar.

'You look stunning.' He leaned over, placing a kiss on her cheek.

'You clean up rather nicely yourself, Mr Halley.' She smiled, slipping Ayu into gear. 'Are you ok?'

Kerr's hand ran through his hair. 'I think so. You?'

'Yeah... Though I guess you-know-who doesn't know we're doing this together.'

'No, he doesn't. I told him I was busy with Tavrach. Which isn't a lie. There's another gig tomorrow night, but I can't avoid telling him forever.'

'I know.' Georgie's heart sank.

'I'm sorry.' Kerr placed his hand over hers. 'I wish there was an easy way to face this. But I don't even know exactly what to tell him.'

'I don't know either. I'd like to apologise to him, but if I do that now, it'll look like I'm doing it as a prelude to saying, "so I hope you're ok with that because I'm dating your brother now".'

'It sucks, doesn't it? I hate walking on eggshells like this.'

'Then how about we tell him together?'

'Yeah, ok. When did you have in mind?'

'Would you like to wait until the music festival is done? Next Saturday is the last night, isn't it?'

He nodded.

'Then how about the Sunday? We can go and see him. And you'll be back at school the next day, so you can avoid him.'

Kerr smirked. 'Good thinking.'

Fairy lights hung from the ceiling of the hotel ballroom like captured stars as they entered along with some other evening guests. Georgie stood at the edge of the dance floor, champagne flute in hand, watching as Hayley twirled in her husband's arms. 'She looks amazing.' Radiant, in fact, in her beaded ivory satin fishtail gown, her elaborate updo perfectly intact despite hours of celebration. Hayley laughed as Oliver whispered something in her ear, and the sound carried across the room – pure, uncomplicated joy.

A sharp, unexpected pang of envy needled Georgie. Not for the wedding itself – she'd never been the type to fantasise about white dresses and first dances – but for the certainty that radiated from the couple. They knew where they belonged: with each other.

Georgie had tasted a fleeting sense of that since her return to Glenbriar, but it felt too flimsy to guarantee it lasting.

Oliver led Hayley in a gentle spin, his kilt swinging as they moved across the polished floor.

'They suit each other,' Kerr smiled, his eyes tracking the newlyweds.

Georgie took a sip of champagne. 'Don't they just.'

'Shall we dance too?' Kerr tilted his head and held out his hand.

Wordlessly, she placed her champagne on a nearby table and let him lead her towards the dance floor.

The band shifted to a slower number, something soft and romantic that had couples drawing closer together. Kerr's hand settled at her waist, warm through the satin of her dress. His other hand held hers against his chest, where the steady rhythm of his heartbeat.

'You look beautiful tonight,' he murmured. 'You always do. I don't know how you do it in that little campervan.'

'I was thinking that myself earlier. It's starting to feel too small. I think the honeymoon with Ayu is over.'

He raised his chin slightly. 'I see.'

The fairy lights spun above them as they turned, creating patterns that matched the fluttering in Georgie's chest. Other couples moved around them – Elise with Gabe, Genevieve with Finlay, and the two other bridesmaids with their partners.

'I hope Jake listens to what we have to say,' she said, the words barely audible over the music.

Kerr's hand tightened slightly at her waist. 'I hope so too, but I'm not confident. Eddie reckons Jake likes having something to be angry about, and I see what he means. I think my parents are a bit scared of him… or what he might do. I kind of wonder if it's always been like that.'

'I think he has.' She met his eyes. 'I definitely found him hard work. And I was scared to upset him because I always felt like he had the capacity to hurt himself.'

'Thing is, when you did split up with him, he didn't actually harm himself, he just got really angry and low. When I...' he swallowed, and his Adam's apple bobbed '...had a really bad split a few years ago, Jake was really kind to me. And he can be, but so often he's angry and self-destructing all over the place... making everyone else feel bad about it.'

'I still want to apologise to him, but I don't know how we can ever explain what's happening here without making everything worse.'

Kerr stopped dancing, though his arms remained around her. The music continued, other couples still swirling past, but they stood motionless. 'Worse for him maybe. But hopefully better for us.'

She rose onto her toes and kissed him. Not a dramatic, sweeping kiss that would draw gasps from the wedding guests – especially not with Kerr's colleague Finlay nearby – but a soft, deliberate meeting of lips. Brief, but intimate enough to leave no doubt where her heart was.

The song ended, transitioning into something more upbeat. Couples around them adjusted, breaking apart or changing their hold, but Georgie and Kerr remained as they were for a moment longer.

'Another dance?' Kerr asked.

'In a minute,' Georgie said. 'I should say hi to some people.'

The bridesmaids had returned to their table with their partners and were laughing and chattering. Elise spotted them approaching, waving them over. The others turned at her signal, Genevieve with her baby bump draped elegantly in navy satin matching the two others, who Georgie didn't immediately recognise.

'Hey.' Elise gave her a hug. 'Good to see you. And Kerr, hi.'

He gave her a little wave, and Georgie remembered that Elise worked with Kerr's mum. Would they talk about it at work? Did Kerr mind his mum finding out? Would it make everything even more awkward with Jake if he found out from someone else first? Hopefully they would get to Jake before that happened.

Georgie smiled as they indicated for her and Kerr to take a seat. Beside Elise sat Gabe, his arm draped casually across the back of her chair.

'Hey, Kerr.' Finlay waved to him. 'I didn't know you were coming.'

'I...um...'

'I forgot the two of you worked with Finlay,' Genevieve said to Kerr.

Kerr and Finlay started chatting about something while Elise gestured to a petite woman with a cascade of ginger curls. 'Have you met Lilah? She's married to Aidan here, who's Hayley's cousin.' Elise gave Georgie a private – slightly weirded-out – look, and Georgie guessed Aidan was the cousin Elise had infamously been engaged to.

'Hi,' Lilah said.

'And this is Willow,' Elise continued, indicating the blonde woman beside Lilah. 'Hayley's other cousin, who we only get to see when she's not busy being Rocky Rainman.'

Georgie's brow furrowed in confusion. 'Isn't that a weatherman?'

'That's me,' Willow said. 'Rocky Rainman is my professional persona.'

The man beside her, who looked like an Italian model, smiled. 'She doesn't really need that alias anymore. It was really only to annoy me that she had it.'

'Because you're on the TV.' Recognition dawned on Georgie. He was Marcus Bowman, a well-known Scottish forecaster. 'In fact aren't you both on TV?'

'We are,' Marcus said. 'We present *Destination Forecast* together.'

'Ah, yes. I've seen it a few times. My mum loves it.'

'Have you two been together long?' Lilah asked, her eyes moving between Georgie and Kerr.

'Um... We're just here casually,' she said. 'I mean... I don't live her permanently.'

'I see,' Lilah said. 'Where do you normally live?'

'In London.'

'She's a famous tennis player,' Elise said.

'Oh?' Lilah pulled a face. 'Sorry, I had no idea. I never watch tennis.'

'It's fine,' Georgie said. 'I've retired now anyway.'

'What do you do now then?' Lilah smiled, and it was clearly an innocent and well-meaning question. But Georgie didn't know what to say. Because despite her month up here searching for peace, she still didn't have a clue.

'I'm considering a few options. I haven't decided yet.' But soon she'd have to. She couldn't live in the van much longer without going crazy.

And with Jake back in Glenbriar, maybe the time to move on was now. The idea of apologising now seemed crazy.

This, however, was the pattern of her life – pack up, move on. Tennis had made it necessary; now it was simply the path of least resistance. Staying would mean breaking that pattern, facing the mess, potentially watching both brothers suffer because of her.

'They're about to cut the cake,' Genevieve announced, pulling Georgie from her spiralling thoughts. 'Bridesmaids, come on.'

The table began to empty, partners helping each other up, gathering purses and jackets, moving towards the centre of the room where Hayley and Oliver awaited with a towering white cake. Kerr stood and offered his hand to Georgie.

She took his hand and let him pull her up. To anyone watching, she looked like she belonged – standing beside a good man, celebrating the joy around them. But under the surface, she was already scanning for exits. Calculating how far she'd have to fall when it all went wrong. Because it always did when her heart got involved.

Chapter Twenty-Two

Kerr

The night air kissed their skin as Kerr and Georgie made their way across the courtyard at Thistle Lodge towards the car park where Ayu was waiting.

'I'm so tired.' Georgie yawned. 'It must be after midnight.'

Kerr pulled out his phone. 'Yeah. It's twenty to one.'

'Aw man, I am not used to this.' She flapped her hand in front of her mouth.

'I thought you would be. Didn't you have late night matches on tour?'

'Oh, I did. And I didn't like them either. Not when my coach was badgering me to be up early to train, my manager was determined for me to get up early for interviews, and I quite often had jetlag. It could be exhausting. That's the bits the fans don't see. They expect to see the best version of you the second you step on court, but they have no idea what led up to that moment.'

'I can see there's a lot of it you won't miss.'

She yawned again. 'Bits of it. But when you get used to it, it's just what you do. Adrenaline carries you a lot of the time and I kind of miss that. The excitement. The thrill.'

He put his arm around her shoulder and gently squeezed it. 'I guess Glenbriar is a bit too run of the mill.'

'It's different, but it has its moments.'

She unlocked the van, and they jumped inside. Kerr looked around the tiny space. 'At least we're not soaking wet this time.'

'Very true.' She took his hand. 'And it's ok if we cuddle this time, isn't it? We don't have to do it to keep warm.'

'Well, we can do it to keep warm, but we can also do it because we want to.'

She slung her arms around his neck. 'I definitely want to.'

Kerr's hands found her waist, pulled her close, bringing them chest to chest, and lowered his mouth to hers. Her lips parted beneath his. Moments ago, the idea of crashing on the bed and sleeping had been all he wanted to do, but his body had sprung back to life. Sleep now felt like a by-product of something a lot sweeter.

They closed all the curtains, then undressed each other with unhurried tenderness. His shirt fell, then his trousers, her underwear following until nothing separated them but the charged air between their bodies. The van wasn't warm, so they tumbled onto the bed, pulling the duvet around them, continuing the kiss until the heat was scorching.

Georgie's body welcomed him almost lazily, her sighs and whispered encouragements guiding him as he worshipped her with fingers and lips. She arched her back when he found a sensitive spot, and her breath caught when he lingered at the inside of her thigh.

Everything was exactly right.

Her leg hooked around his hip, drawing him closer. The sensation of her body accepting his, warm and perfect, eased his heart, and he relaxed into the moment.

As they moved together, Kerr lowered his forehead to hers, and time slowed as the pleasure built between them. None of it was rushed. It felt like they had all the time in the world, though who knew if that was true? Georgie had said her campervan trip was almost over. What did she plan to do now... and would a discussion with Jake fast-track her into a decision? One that meant she wouldn't want to stay here? Kerr's heart crumpled at the thought.

He cupped her face and kissed her hard.

'Oh, Kerr,' she breathed, and her body tightened around his.

He drove deeper, stronger, until he wasn't sure where he ended and she began. She let out a soft cry against his shoulder, her body trembling beneath his, and he followed, unable to hold back as waves of emotion ripped through him.

After disposing of the condom, they curled up together, tangled under the duvet, Georgie's head resting on his chest. Kerr stroked her hair, feeling its silk between his fingertips. His heart was so full, almost overflowing, but the binding holding it together was fragile. Any moment now, it could be ripped from him, and he'd fall apart.

He let out a long sigh and held her close. If he only had now, he had to make the most of it.

Spending Saturday with Georgie was Kerr's preferred option, but she was taking another tennis class in the afternoon, and Kerr was doing another gig with Tavrach that evening. But half term went on for another week, so at least he'd have more time to see her... assuming the meeting with Jake didn't scare her away.

Kerr still hadn't been to see Jake since he'd been back. If he called around casually, he could gauge the mood before they dropped the bomb next week.

As soon as he was showered, he walked the familiar route to his parents' house, hands deep in his jacket pockets, his thoughts dragging behind each step.

He turned the corner past the manse at the top of Kirk Lane and carried on up a wider road that rose quite steeply and led to Arden Crescent.

Delicious cooking smells wafted out as he stepped up to the front door. Mum and Dad had no doubt decided to celebrate having both their sons home with a big tasty lunch. Kerr wouldn't complain, though his insides were a little too knotted to feel particularly hungry.

He opened the door and called, 'Hello, anyone home?'

From the kitchen, his dad's voice drifted out. 'We're all here. In you come.'

Kerr stepped inside, closing the door behind him. With a steadying breath, he moved through to the kitchen.

Jake was already sitting at the table, pint in hand, eyes flicking up as Kerr entered.

'Alright?' Jake said.

Kerr nodded. 'Alright.'

Mum came over and gave him a one-armed hug. 'We've made a roast lunch. It kind of feels like Christmas having you both here.'

'So, how's it hanging, little bro?' Jake swigged some of his pint.

'Fine, yeah. I, um...' He didn't want to return the question, knowing that Jake's life was far from fine. If it was, he wouldn't be here. 'Was your flight ok?'

'Na, it was the usual shit. Delayed. The passenger next to me was a pain, and the food was inedible. I'm not sure why they even bother feeding you on short flights like that.'

Kerr nodded, catching the briefest glance between his parents that seemed to indicate that Jake had been in a similarly negative mood since he got home and nothing seemed to be changing it.

Their position wasn't one Kerr envied. When Jake got into moods like this, it could literally take months to get out of. And when he found out about Kerr and Georgie, it would multiply... In fact, he might never get out of it.

This was what Kerr had to prepare for.

They all took their seats at the table, the clatter of cutlery and chair legs briefly filling the silence.

'We've got beef and chicken.' Dad lifted lids off serving dishes with a flourish like it was a MasterChef final. 'I prefer the beef and Mum likes chicken, so we've hopefully got everyone covered unless either of you has turned vegetarian.'

Jake grunted. 'Whatever, just anything.'

Mum smiled brightly. 'Well, if you have turned veggie, you can have the lemon asparagus. I love it. It's my new addiction.'

'I'm not sure I want to ask what your last one was.' Kerr took a slice of chicken, then passed the dish on. He kept his gaze on his plate, resisting the urge to glance at Jake again. The mood in the room had the weight of a storm front. You could ignore it all you wanted – the grey clouds, the thick air – but the lightning was going to hit whether you looked up or not.

'There's roasties, mash, and that squash stuff you liked the last time you were here, Jake.' Mum spooned a generous helping onto her plate. 'I got that sticky toffee pudding you used to love for afters.'

Jake shrugged. 'Did I? Can't say I remember ever liking that.'

'Well, I'll eat it if you don't want it.' Dad carved a thick slice of beef. 'It's delicious.'

'This is great, thanks, exalted-parental ones,' Kerr said.

Jake snorted. 'Yeah, thanks. But I'm not sure we need this much food on a daily basis.'

Mum gave a forced chuckle. 'It's just a treat for today, while we have you both here.'

Jake didn't even crack a smile.

Kerr forced down a mouthful of mash that suddenly felt like glue. This wasn't new. Jake had always had these spirals – these dark, biting moods where everything tasted sour and no conversation made it past his wall of pessimism. His refusal to get help hurt not just himself but the whole family. Kate and Douglas were good parents, but now they treated Jake like an unexploded bomb.

'How was the festival?' Mum said after a pause to Kerr. 'Were you at a gig last night?'

'No. It was open-mic night last night. I don't do anything for that.' He carefully avoided mentioning the wedding. 'But Tavrach have their gig at the Cross Keys tonight. It's not a bad day, so they'll probably get outside. Then I'm doing the closing gig for them next Saturday at the pink hotel.'

'What are you on about?' Jake muttered. 'Have you got a new job or something? Nobody frigging tells me anything.'

Mum's fork paused mid-air. 'It's not a new job. Kerr's helping out with the sound at the Autumn Gold Festival.'

Jake picked up his pint and took a long drink. 'What even is that?'

'A music festival around Glenbriar.' Kerr speared a carrot.

'You should go along to one of their gigs.' Dad pointed at Jake. 'You used to be a big music fan. You even had us buy that drum kit one year.'

'That's right.' Mum pulled a face, then smiled. 'Why don't you do that? Go along to one of the gigs? You could meet up with some of your old friends. Have some fun. It'll take your mind off things.'

'Something tells me that's not going to work.' Jake's scowl deepened. 'My fiancée's been cheating on me, I've lost my home, and I'm stuck here. I don't see that a night listening to some local band is really going to help.'

The table fell silent.

'No one expects these little things to change everything,' Mum said finally. 'It's a distraction.'

'I'm not sure I want to be distracted,' Jake replied. 'None of you understand what it's like to have someone you trusted completely betray you.'

Kerr's stomach twisted. If Jake only knew.

'Oh, we do,' Dad said gently. 'No one goes through life without some kind of hurt. It might not be exactly the same or to the same level, but of course we understand.'

'And isn't distraction better than wallowing?' Kerr said, only just stopping himself from adding 'in self-pity'.

Jake's jaw worked as he chewed a potato. 'Can we just eat? Without the amateur psychology?'

Kerr held his breath, trying to focus on his food. If Jake was this bad already, god only knew what would happen when he found out about Kerr and Georgie.

Chapter Twenty-Three

Georgie

Georgie slapped away a backhand, her favourite shot from her tour days. Kerr lunged for it but could only clip it with the edge of his racquet.

'You're ferocious, aren't you?'

She giggled and picked up another ball.

Both of them knew the risks of meeting up in Glenbriar now that Jake was back, though he was working from his parents' house and was unlikely to be wandering around the town. The courts seemed like a safe option though. Jake hadn't played tennis since he was overlooked for the junior team all those years ago. And since the split with Georgie, he actively detested the sport, so he was unlikely to show up here.

Georgie served a ball to Kerr. She had a funny feeling he wasn't avoiding Jake just because of her. From what he'd mentioned about Jake, it sounded like he was not in a good place... or mood.

They hit some more balls. Kerr wasn't a stylish player, but when his timing was accurate, he could generate a good amount of power. Which Georgie appreciated because hard hitting was always good therapy and helped get rid of restless energy, which she had a lot of right now.

After an hour, they headed back to the clubhouse for a cold drink.

'After the final gig of the Autumn Festival...' Georgie swigged back some water. 'I really need to decide what I'm doing. I want to see the closing night, but I don't think I can stay in the van any longer. It's driving me mad now.'

Kerr ran his fingers through his hair. 'Listen, I hope you don't think I'm being rude or inconsiderate not asking if you want to stay with me for a bit. I mean, it's early days, but—'

'No Kerr.' She held up her hand. 'I don't think that at all. I guess my future plans are a mystery to everyone... including myself.'

'Well... Are you planning on sticking around?'

'I want to, but...'

Her phone rang, and she glanced at it, wishing she hadn't. Martin Harlow, her former agent, who seemed to be desperate to take her on again and who was now constantly emailing her opportunities he thought would be perfect for her. But to actually call her... What was this all about?

'Two minutes.' She pulled an apologetic face at Kerr. 'Martin,' she answered. 'Is everything ok?'

'Of course. How are you? Are you back from your trip yet?'

'Not yet.'

'Ah, well. You maybe haven't had a chance to check your emails, but I really would like to urge you to consider the commentary opportunity for the tour finals. This could get you back in business and put you in an excellent place for starting next year. I'm pretty sure I could get you the Australian Open, and as soon as you have a slam under your belt, I don't think there will be any difficulty in getting you Wimbledon.'

Georgie's heart skipped. Wimbledon. The tournament that had defined so much of her career, her dreams, her identity. She'd never succeeded in winning it, but commentary jobs there were almost as prestigious.

'I... um.' She glanced up at Kerr. He was busying himself with opening an energy snack, but she was pretty sure he was listening. 'I'll have to think about it.'

'Not too long. I can give you a week. No more.'

'Ok. I'll let you know.' She said goodbye and ended the call.

'That sounded promising.' Kerr smiled at her, but she knew it was only on the surface. His eyes were dull. 'Does that help you decide what you want to do next?'

She nodded. Yes. Wasn't this exactly what she needed? Something concrete. She would have a schedule again, be back on the tour. Ok, it would be in a different capacity, but it would be familiar. It would pay the bills and give her financial security.

A surge of pain shot up her throat, and she turned away from Kerr in case it manifested as tears. Maybe she did belong on the tour, but her heart belonged next to his. That was where she felt happiest.

'Good morning, you two.' The door opened, and Amanda came in slightly breathless. 'This is good timing. I was going to ring you both to see if you were free.' She craned her neck to look out of the window. 'I've put the kids on the court. I hope they're not arguing.'

'What did you want us for?' Kerr asked.

'I've printed five copies of the application for the MUGA funding.' Amanda opened her bag and pulled out some papers. 'I just wanted you to read it over before I send it, and Georgie, is it definitely ok to use your name as an endorsement? I think it'll really help to have that kind of backing.'

'Yeah, sure.' Georgie flipped the paper over. 'I'll always support community sports projects in Glenbriar.' Though it was looking more and more likely that she'd be supporting them from London and not in the town itself.

The Loch View Hotel was locally known as the pink hotel, for obvious reasons. It was a stunning place, especially when all decked out in lights for the closing of the Autumn Gold Festival. There was also a forest light show here, which made this time of year very popular in Glenbriar for both tourists and locals. And the hotel was already packed as Georgie parked in the car park.

Kerr would already be inside helping to set up, and Georgie had arranged to sit with Elise again as Gabe was also performing.

Tables were clustered around the small stage, and the bar was already three-deep with festival-goers ordering pre-performance drinks.

'Georgie!' Elise waved across the crowded room from a table near the wall. Beside her sat a striking young woman Georgie didn't recognise, with her vibrant red hair styled in an elaborate updo, multiple earrings climbing the curve of one ear, and a band t-shirt beneath a leather jacket decorated with pins and patches. Despite the edgy appearance, there was something subdued in the way she hunched slightly over her drink, eyes downcast.

Georgie threaded her way through the crowd, nodding to some familiar faces. How quickly she'd got to know people. There was Logan, the campsite owner, Eddie Caldwell, and a couple she recognised from Hayley's wedding – Ophelia, Hayley's very glamourous friend, with her builder boyfriend, who seemed to catch many eyes.

'How are you?' Elise stood to greet her with a quick hug.

'Good, thanks.' Georgie put her clutch on the table and adjusted the edge of her off-shoulder cream sweater. 'Though I'm glad I got a ticket. It's packed in here.'

'Sure is.' Elise gestured to the redhead beside her. 'This is Scarlett, by the way. Scarlett, Georgie Porter.'

'Hi.' Scarlett offered a slight smile.

'Let me get us some drinks.' Elise got to her feet. 'What can I get you both?'

They gave their orders, and Elise headed for the bar.

'Elise said you're a tennis player, right?' Scarlett said.

'I was.' Georgie nodded. 'I retired earlier in the year.'

'Ah, right. So what do you do now?'

'Um... I might be going into commentary. What about you? What do you do?'

'This and that.' Scarlett gave a little shrug. 'None of the jobs I've had have really been me.'

'That's a shame. What would be your dream job?'

Scarlett huffed out a laugh. 'I really have no idea.'

'Same,' Georgie said. 'I guess I've done my dream job and now I don't have a clue what to do next. I love books, so maybe I can work in a library or something.'

'Maybe,' Scarlett said. 'What kind of books do you read?'

'Romances are my favourite. One that I was reading inspired me to get a campervan and come up here.'

'Really?' Scarlett raised an eyebrow. 'Do you actually believe romance is real?'

'I'd like to.'

'I guess it sounds nice, but it also seems a matter of luck.'

Georgie looked around, checking for any sign of Kerr, but she didn't see him. Eddie smiled at her from a table nearby. Other people were arriving and sitting next to him – mostly women.

They obviously knew him and were greeting him and hugging him.

'Oh god.' Scarlett put her head down. 'That's Mr Caldwell. He used to be my teacher. And that's Miss Bonham.'

Georgie followed Scarlett's sightline to a very glam woman who looked to be in her mid-thirties. She wore a figure-hugging leopard-print wrap dress, gold heels, and a black wrap. Her black hair was styled in loose curls, and she had on deep red lipstick that made her smile look very wide as she laughed and joked with Eddie.

'Was she your teacher too?'

'Yeah, she's a geography teacher. I hope she doesn't see me.'

'Why? Isn't she nice?' She looked very friendly from here.

'Na, she's really nice, but she'll probably want to know my life story if she comes over... And I don't exactly have one.'

'Oh dear.' Georgie sucked on her lip. Maybe the people sitting with Eddie were all teachers. Kerr's colleagues perhaps.

Elise returned with drinks and took her seat again.

'Two secs.' Scarlett got up. 'I'm bursting for the loo.'

'Who is she?' Georgie asked.

'She's Aidan's sister.'

'Aidan? Your ex.'

'Yeah. I know. It's mental. But we all ended up on a coach trip this summer, and she's been going through a really hard time. She had a bad breakup a few months ago. The guy was a real piece of work. I just feel that she needs a friend.'

Georgie nodded. 'Aw, that's sweet of you.'

Her gaze drifted back to the stage area, still searching for Kerr. Why did relationships hurt so much? Why did people keep trying, knowing the statistical likelihood of failure, of heartbreak? Her parents had somehow managed it – thirty-plus years together. But they seemed increasingly like outliers in a world where commitment had become temporary, conditional, revocable.

How did anyone stay together? Or find the right person in the first place? What if you found the right person but didn't know what to do next? A career move or a love affair? The feminist part of her brain said to choose the career... The romantic side said to choose love.

Scarlett returned and went straight to her drink.

The lights dimmed slightly, and a woman stepped onto the stage to announce the first performer. Georgie's attention split between the stage and the continued scanning of the room for Kerr. She finally spotted the top of his head behind a screen made of equipment.

The first notes of an acoustic guitar filled the room, and Georgie sank into contemplation as the music started. Relationships, careers, homes – all requiring decisions, commitments, the courage to say 'this one' instead of keeping all doors perpetually open or moving from place to place. Martin was waiting for her answer. Kerr was stuck in an ugly situation with his brother. And she was here, still completely uncertain about what to do next.

The music swelled around her. Adam, the Tavrach frontman, sang in his low, raspy voice.

I stood at the edge where the road split wide,
Heart in my mouth, truth I couldn't hide.
One path was safe, the other was wild,
I took one step – scared but alive.

He lowered his head, and his hair fell over his eyes as he strummed, then he went on.

They'll say I was reckless, they'll say I was wrong,
But silence is louder when you wait too long.

Georgie tapped her foot as the beat picked up, surging into the chorus.

It's not the ability to choose perfectly,
But the courage to choose at all –
To risk the fall.
I didn't know what the end would be,
I just knew I had to stand tall.
I made my move,
Now I've gotta live with whatever comes after–
The heartbreak, the laughter...
The courage to choose.

Was that the secret? Not the ability to choose perfectly, but the courage to choose at all? And to live with that choice through whatever came after?

Chapter Twenty-Four

Kerr

Kerr adjusted the balance on the sound desk, nudging the bass down a notch as the second verse kicked in. The acoustics in the room were decent, better than he'd expected considering Adam's critique of it at their first meeting.

Kerr kept half an eye on Adam, who leaned into the mic like he was bleeding the lyrics. Moving almost automatically, Kerr tweaked a slider here, faded in a backing track there.

His gaze wandered and, like it had been called there, found Georgie. She wore a pale sweater that slipped off one shoulder. Her hair was loose, glossy, and amazingly styled. Her profile angled towards the stage, lips parted slightly as she listened.

He swept the room again, checking volume levels and speaker range. In the middle, Eddie held court at a round table. All around him sat colleagues from school, eating up his charm as always.

When Tavrach were done, they moved off stage for the first open-mic session. Kerr wasn't needed for this bit, so he slipped into the packed function room.

Clara waved to him straight away like she'd been watching for him. He smiled and scanned the rest of the table. Mirren was there, presumably to watch Benji. Brenna was also there, looking ridiculously glam as always, and Polly Ritchie, the young biology teacher.

'Ladies.' He approached their table.

'Not funny.' Eddie folded his arms.

'You didn't wait for me to finish. I was going to say, "and gentleman".'

Eddie winked at him.

'So, is everyone having fun?'

Clara's face lit up, her hands immediately gesturing to an empty chair. 'Join us. We're having a staff night out.'

He perched on the edge of the seat.

'I can't believe the holidays are nearly over already,' Brenna moaned.

'Same,' Polly added.

'I miss Lissa,' Clara said.

'Me too.' Brenna sipped her drink. 'But her baby is so sweet she might not want to come back. Having said that, I'm glad I'm out of that stage, though to be honest, it's easy compared to the grumpy eleven-year-old I have now.'

Kerr's attention drifted until his gaze landed on Georgie.

His heart stuttered, then raced. One day without seeing her felt like weeks.

'Earth to Kerr.' Clara's voice broke through his trance. 'We've lost you to the crowd, I see.'

He blinked, returning his attention to the table with an apologetic smile. 'Sorry. I just can't believe how many people are here tonight.'

Clara's gaze followed his previous line of sight, landing on Georgie. When she looked back at Kerr, something had shifted in her expression. 'Isn't that the tennis player who you said came around your door a while back?'

'Oh... um, yeah.'

'Is she living here now?'

'Not sure.'

'Don't suppose you could grab me some crisps from the bar?' Eddie said.

Kerr looked at him and, when their eyes met, Eddie silently indicated that the crisps were merely an escape route if Kerr wanted it.

'Sure, what flavour?'

'You choose... and no rush if you want to speak to anyone else on the way.'

As Kerr passed the back of Eddie's chair, he ruffled Eddie's hair. 'Thanks, mate,' he mumbled. With a quick glance back, he waved to the table at large. Clara's eyes followed him, that same unreadable expression. Why was she looking at him like that? She was a nice person, and the look wasn't threatening, but it was piercing... Was she concerned about something?

He pushed the thought aside and headed over to Georgie's table.

'Hi,' he said as he reached her.

Elise and Georgie looked up. The redhead they were sharing the table with gave him the side-eye through her dramatic eyeliner. Her outfit wouldn't have looked amiss on the stage.

'You enjoying it?' Kerr sat on a chair. 'It's looking to be a great night.'

'That was such a great new song,' Elise said.

Kerr grinned. 'Yeah, it was.'

'This should be good.' Elise sat back as a man got up on the stage to loud cheers and whistles.

'He's the builder, isn't he?' Georgie asked.

'Oh god,' the redhead muttered. 'My mum fancies him.'

Kerr laughed. 'I think mine does too.'

'I think half the town does,' Elise said.

A ripple of excited murmurs swept through the room as Brann took the stage with his guitar and smiled. 'Hey. It's me again. Thought I'd do a cover today. See if you recognise it. I've shaken it up a bit.' He began to play; his voice was a little rough around the edges, but very tuneful.

As the song progressed, Kerr's gaze drifted across the room. His eyes landed on his colleagues' table and found Clara watching him, her expression thoughtful and slightly sad. When their eyes met, she didn't look away but offered a small smile.

Kerr returned it before looking away. He'd worked with Clara for a while now, but something seemed off.

When Brann finished, everyone clapped and cheered. Kerr checked his watch. 'Twenty minutes before I'm on again.'

Georgie smiled at him. 'Do you want to get some air?'

'Yeah, just for five minutes. I don't want to wander too far.'

'We can just stand out the front.'

'Ok.'

As they stood, Kerr caught Clara's eye across the room again, but she blinked and looked away as if to pretend she hadn't been looking at all.

The night was cool on his cheeks as they stepped outside, the sounds of the festival fading behind the glass door of the Loch View's front exit. Beside him, Georgie seemed to unfurl slightly.

'I feel like I've been holding my breath all night,' she said.

'Why?' He leaned in and kissed her on the lips. Georgie's arms wrapped around his neck, pulling him closer until they were pressed together from chest to knee.

'I don't know. I just feel a bit lost. But... that song. Did you listen to the lyrics?'

'Which one?'

'Tavrach's new song.'

His hand traced the line of her spine through her top. 'Yeah, it was good.'

'The lyrics.' She stopped and swallowed. Voices were coming across the car park. It sounded like latecomers or perhaps a group who'd been out for a smoke.

Kerr moved Georgie over to the edge of the stairs, so they could easily get past.

'What about the lyrics?'

'Well, they were about choices, and I thought—'

'What the hell is this?' a painfully familiar voice said.

Kerr went rigid, his body turning to stone beneath Georgie's touch. No. It couldn't be. Not here, not now.

'Shit.' Kerr breathed. His mind raced frantically, cataloguing possible escapes that didn't exist. They literally had nowhere to go. Jake and a friend were standing right in front of them.

'Jake.' Kerr stepped out of Georgie's embrace. 'You said you weren't interested in the festival. I didn't expect to see you here.'

Jake stood frozen, eyes moving between Kerr and Georgie. His friend sensed the sudden tension, his laughter dying as he glanced between Jake and Kerr.

'Clearly,' Jake said, the single word like ice.

'Listen—'

'I don't think so,' Jake said. 'It seems I've been missing out on all sorts of interesting developments.'

The brothers stared at each other across the steps, neither moving, neither speaking. In the heavy silence, Kerr's own heart beat so loudly it could have rivalled the Tavrach drummer.

'You need to let me speak,' Kerr said.

Jake shook his head, staring at Georgie. 'This is all because of you. All of it.' His eyes flicked back to Kerr. 'First me, now you. She's pulled a number on both of us, and you've fallen into her trap.'

Kerr's insides turned over. Nothing he did or said now could get him out of this situation without a fight.

Chapter Twenty-Five

Georgie

Jake and Kerr stared at each other, both tense, their faces serious, and the air charged with the weight of the history she'd helped create. If it wasn't for her, these two brothers might be here together, both with their own partners – not conflicted because of one woman.

Jake's friend lingered, exchanging an uncomfortable glance with Georgie. 'Is everything ok, Jake?'

Jake ignored him, his focus laser-sharp on Georgie. His jaw worked beneath his skin, the controlled anger more frightening than outright rage would have been. Georgie's throat felt tight, her pulse hammering in her ears.

'We were going to tell you. Can we talk somewhere more private?' she asked.

'Talk?' Jake repeated the word like it tasted foul. 'I already told Kerr I never want to talk to you again. And now, instead of saying fine and leaving, you're still here. And not just still here. You're here with your claws in my brother. You can't get what you want from me, so you've resorted to something low. Typical Georgie.'

Kerr moved slightly, positioning himself more firmly between them. 'Jake, that's not what happened.'

'Don't you start.' Jake's voice rose. 'I know what she is and what she's done to you, but really for you to go along with it.' He ran his hand through his hair and shook his head. His expression looked like he was in agony. Georgie's heart contracted. This was everything she'd dreaded – and then some.

'She hasn't done anything *to* me,' Kerr said. 'You're upset, I get that. But you really should listen.'

Jake's friend had drifted towards the hotel entrance, clearly uncomfortable with the family drama unfolding.

'Why the hell should I?' Jake's attention shifted fully to Georgie; his hazel eyes were so similar to Kerr's but lacking their warmth. 'I've heard it all before. Every excuse under the sun.'

'Jake, stop,' Kerr said. Georgie placed a hand on his arm, steadying herself as much as him.

'You haven't heard anything.' She met Jake's gaze despite the guilt churning in her stomach. 'I never told you what happened or how sorry I am.'

'The sympathy apology, too late after the fact.' Jake shook his head. 'I know why you did everything. You're an egocentric piece of work. It's all about you. It always was.'

Each word landed like a punch. Was it? She was perfectly happy to take the blame for her part in this, but had she warped *his* part in her mind? Was he innocent? When he'd refused to break up when she left, she didn't have the strength to insist.

She'd done everything he wanted – well, until he'd wanted to get physical. And she couldn't. She'd drawn a line, made excuses. Because deep down, she hadn't wanted to be with him at all.

'Don't speak to her like that, Jake. From where she's standing it probably looks like it was all about you,' Kerr said.

'Seriously?' Jake glared at him.

'Maybe it was my fault,' she said. 'I definitely made mistakes. And I am truly sorry for the impact it's had on you.'

'Nothing you say or do can ever make up for it.'

'Come on, Jake.' Kerr threw his hands out. 'Cut her some slack. She's trying to apologise and make things right. How can you say she's egocentric when you're the one refusing to listen or to hear the other side of the story?'

'Because I don't care what she's doing. If you really want to make things right.' He turned back to her. 'Then leave. Go away and don't darken our doors anymore. It took me long enough to deal with your shit the last time. I don't need it again, especially now when so much other crap is going on.'

His words stole her breath. What had she expected? Whatever it was, this was much worse. Maybe he was right. What if the only sensible thing to do here was leave?

'I'm going in,' Jake said. 'I've already missed quite a bit.' He glared at Kerr, then flicked his eyes back to Georgie. 'You better keep away from me. Keep away from my whole family.' He turned and stormed up the stairs.

'Are you ok?' Kerr put his arms around her.

'I think so.' But she wasn't sure. Causing a rift like this in a family wasn't what she wanted. And if she was with Kerr, could she avoid Jake indefinitely? 'Don't you have to go in too?' She pulled back to look at him. 'For the band.'

He checked his phone. 'Yeah, but I don't want to leave you.'

Georgie stepped out of his hold. 'You go. I just need a moment.'

Kerr hesitated. 'Ok. As soon as I've done the next section, I'll find you.' He leaned over and kissed her cheek.

'I'm sorry, Kerr,' she said.

'What for?' He gave her an agonised look.

'Messing up your family again.'

'Don't say that. I'll speak to him again. As often as I have to. He doesn't get to talk to you like that.'

'You better go.'

'Ok. Please, don't stay out here too long.'

But Georgie wasn't going back in. She couldn't now that she knew Jake was in there. Who knew what he'd do if he saw her?

She walked to the edge of the car park, away from the hotel, where a path all decorated in fairy lights led to the loch. Inside, the music had started again, and she heard the reverb even from out here.

There was really only one answer. The only way she could avoid breaking up the Halley family was if she kept away from them, like Jake said. If she stayed here, these kinds of fights would happen over and over again, no matter what she said or how much Kerr intervened.

She thought of Martin's call, the commentary job waiting for her decision. That was where the road was leading her. This had just been a detour. The fleeting happiness she'd had with Kerr was something to add to the memory bank, just like winning tournaments, defeating a top seed, and winning a bronze medal at the Olympics were. All memories. That was where Kerr belonged.

The night air bit at her cheeks, her inadequate off-shoulder sweater offering little protection against the autumn chill. With a deep breath, she turned and marched across the car park towards Ayu. She'd only had a mocktail to drink, knowing she'd be driving back tonight, though she hadn't expected it to be so soon.

Starting the engine, she drove towards Heather Glen. The campsite was quiet at this hour, most occupants either still out enjoying the festival or already tucked into bed. A few windows glowed in the caravans, rectangles of warm light that made the surrounding darkness feel more complete.

There was nothing to stop her from just driving away. She could head back to London right now. But good sense told her to at least wait until morning when she'd rested. And rest was all it would be, because she knew she wouldn't sleep a wink.

Sinking onto the bench seat, not bothering to turn on the light, she sat in the darkness. Her breathing sounded too loud, too intrusive in the small space. Her phone buzzed in her pocket, and she pulled it out, squinting at the screen's sudden brightness.

Three messages from Elise:

Where are you??

Everything ok?

Getting worried. Text me!

One from Kerr:

Are you still outside? I don't see you with Elise. x

Her chest squeezed. *Shit*. She'd left without a word to Elise. Her fingers tapped out a reply.

Sorry for disappearing. Started feeling ill. I'm going to sleep it off. Nothing serious, just needed quiet. Talk tomorrow. x

She pressed send, then reopened Kerr's message. Whatever she said here would no doubt be completely inadequate.

I needed space, so I left. So sorry, but I really don't think this will work out for us. I'm not prepared to break up your family. I've caused enough hurt already. Doing this by phone is shit. I know that. But I don't think I can actually speak right now. Please forgive and forget me. xx

Tears trickled down her face as she typed, and she hit send without trying to alter it or filter it. If it was too harsh, too brief, or whatever, so what? Kerr could just add it to her list of faults and, hopefully, it would help him get over her.

She pulled off her clothes and wiped off her makeup before jumping under the covers. As soon as she was there, she let the tears flow, sobbing into her pillow. The knowledge that she'd brought so much of this on herself neither improved nor worsened the situation. It just served as a reminder of human fallibility. Her weak shoulder had been the undoing of her tennis career, and her weak mind had been the undoing of her love life. If she could go back thirteen years to when Jake Halley had asked her out, only three words would have passed her lips.

No, thank you.

Three words that could have prevented all this heartache.

Chapter Twenty-Six

Kerr

Kerr stared at his computer screen. Monday morning and the first day back after half term had arrived, and he was here, but only in body. He'd slept perhaps three hours total, the weekend's chaos replaying in a relentless loop whenever he closed his eyes. Georgie's message. Jake's fury. The gradual understanding that he was losing them both and had no idea how to prevent it. Perhaps he was already too late. Georgie was leaving. Maybe she'd gone already. He didn't even know how to respond to her message. Everything he'd typed seemed hideously inadequate message.

I'm so sorry you feel that way. Obviously, this is not what I hoped for. Will you take the commentary job? If you want to talk, I'll be here. xx

All of stirred up the old feelings of being rejected for a good opportunity. That was what Anna had done – twice. But this was different. Jake's part in it couldn't be overlooked.

'Mr Halley? Can you have a look at this?'

He blinked, suddenly aware of Greig Cormac hovering beside his desk.

'Sure. What is it?'

'Can you check the coding on my design? I can't get it to display a picture even though I've followed all the steps. It just has an empty placeholder.'

'I'll come over.' He got to his feet and followed Greig to his desk.

After spending some time working through the code and the occasional glitches with Greig, the lunch bell rang.

'Ok, folks, we've overrun a bit today, but that means you were all really well engaged, so let's keep that up next lesson.'

Students began packing away with a shuffle of books and a scrape of chairs. Kerr dismissed the class, watching them file out.

'Hello. Oh, Kerr, are you ok? You don't look too clever.'

Clara stopped in the corridor outside his room, her eyes wide with concern. She wore a navy dress cut in a kind of nautical style that looked both professional and soft, her brown hair falling in a neat curtain around her sweet face.

'Yeah... I'm fine.'

She stepped fully into the classroom. 'Were you partying all night on Saturday? That was an amazing gig to end the festival.'

'Um, yeah. I probably stayed out a bit too long. Nothing some coffee won't fix.'

'Hmm.' She tilted her head, studying him. 'Are you sure that's all?'

For a brief, tempting moment, Kerr considered unburdening himself. She was the guidance teacher, after all. Maybe she could give him some. But the thought of saying it all aloud – of admitting how thoroughly he'd messed everything up – was unbearable. If he was going to tell anyone, it needed to be Eddie. He was the one who would listen and not judge. While Clara was a lovely person, she wasn't the person Kerr wanted to confide in.

'I appreciate the concern,' he said finally, 'but I'm fine. Just didn't sleep well.'

Clara's mouth tightened slightly. 'I wonder…' She fiddled with the edge of her collar. 'Would you like to get a drink or something, sometime? Or maybe we could find a gig to go to together, as we both seem to enjoy the same music.'

Kerr's stomach clenched. Shit. Was this why she'd kept looking at him on Saturday? Heat rose up his neck. How could he turn her down without making this awkward? But then, she'd obviously taken a risk asking him at all.

'Listen, I appreciate you asking me. And I would do it as a friend. But… If it's a date, I can't. I'd rather not date a colleague. Sorry.' He pulled a face.

She smiled like it was no big deal, but her eyes told a different story. They looked hopeless and a little sad. 'That's fine. Of course, a drink as friends sometime is all I meant. Though this term gets ridiculously busy with the prelims, then Christmas.'

'Yeah. Doesn't it?'

'Are you coming to the staffroom? You need that coffee after all.'

'Yes, I do. Let's go.'

He walked down with her, not sure what to say, aware of how tall he was and how tiny she was. Everything felt even worse than before. Not only had he lost Georgie, but now he was in a horribly uncomfortable situation with someone he'd always liked and respected.

Eddie was at the door of the staffroom as they entered, chatting with Adele and Brenna, who both looked like they were auditioning for the most glamourous teacher of the year award. He caught Kerr's eye, then smiled at the ladies.

'Kerr, I'm walking to the shop to grab something sweet. It's been one of those mornings – which doesn't bode well for the first day back – but would you like to come with me?'

'Yes, I do.' Kerr didn't hesitate. He not only wanted to speak to Eddie, but he needed to get out of here.

They followed the road that wound around the school's perimeter, autumn leaves crunching beneath their shoes, the October air sharp enough to pink their cheeks. Eddie's stride matched Kerr's – unhurried but purposeful.

'So...' Eddie glanced around, checking no one was within earshot. 'Are you going to tell me what's going on, or shall we pretend this is just a lovely constitutional on a crisp autumn day?'

Kerr glanced sideways at his friend. 'I don't even know where to start.'

'That bad, huh?' Eddie stepped around a large puddle.

A dry laugh escaped Kerr despite himself. 'Worse.'

'Oh dear.' Eddie slowed slightly. 'Out with it then.'

'Ok, well first, Clara just asked me out. And I feel so shit that I turned her down. But I don't like her like that. I mean, I do like her. She's really lovely... but... oh god.'

Eddie put his hand on Kerr's shoulder. 'It's ok. She'll understand. Like you say, she's a lovely person. I was chatting with her a lot on Saturday night, and I think she's feeling a bit lonely. She probably just thought that, as you're both single, she'd take a chance. But she obviously doesn't realise there's someone else on your radar.'

'Yeah, but that's the other problem.'

'Georgie?'

Kerr nodded, then launched into the full story of what had happened with Jake on Saturday night. Eddie listened without interruption, occasionally nodding but mostly just absorbing the tangled narrative. When Kerr finally fell silent, they had reached the small convenience store.

'So she's leaving,' Eddie said, 'and you're letting her go.'

'It's not my choice, is it? I'm not her keeper.'

'True. But tell me, how exactly do you feel about her?'

'What do you mean?' Kerr scraped the sole of his boot across the pavement, not meeting Eddie's eye.

'It's a perfectly simple question.'

'What?'

'Ok, let me put it another way. How much do you like her?'

'How can I measure that?'

'A little, a lot... or like what you've just done with Clara? Enough for her to be a friend, but no more. So tell me about Georgie. Quantify how much you feel for her.'

Kerr pinched the bridge of his nose. 'A lot.'

'Good.' Eddie placed his hand on Kerr's shoulder. 'Enough to fight for.'

Kerr nodded. 'Yes.'

'So what's holding you back?'

'My brother.'

'How?'

'Because if we decide to be together, he'll always be there – even if not physically. He won't let go of how Georgie dumped him. He's obsessed. I don't want to belittle his hurt, but – arrgghh.' He gripped his hair and growled.

'Kerr, you've been hurt in the past too. You had a nightmare breakup, and you got through it. It's easy to use your brother as a shield, so you don't have to face the feelings eating you up. I'm not dismissing your brother's pain. But what they had ended several years ago. Whatever happened between them belongs to the past.'

'Try telling Jake that,' Kerr muttered.

'Jake's responsible for his own healing,' Eddie replied. 'Just as you're responsible for your own happiness. You can't build a future by living in the ruins of someone else's past.'

Kerr closed his eyes and sighed. Jake's bitterness whenever Georgie's name was mentioned, and the way he'd clung to his anger like a life raft was frightening. It was that fear that was keeping Kerr back. Perhaps the same fear that had prevented Georgie from breaking up with him when she left Glenbriar. 'I'm scared of what he might do.'

'I understand. It's not easy. But sometimes you have to feel the fear and do it anyway.'

Kerr smiled. 'That's Georgie's motto.'

'I know it is.' Eddie winked. 'I let someone walk away once.' Eddie's gaze fixed on a parked car. 'Long before I met Kenneth. We had something special – the kind of connection that changes you. But my father was ill, Daniel had an opportunity in London, and I told myself the timing was wrong.' His mouth quirked in a sad approximation of his usual smile. 'I thought I was doing the noble thing, making the selfless choice.'

He turned to Kerr, his eyes reflecting decades-old regret. 'You know what I got for my nobility? Regret, and an empty heart. For years, I wondered what might have happened if I'd asked him to stay or offered to follow him when my father improved. The "what ifs" are brutal, Kerr. They don't fade with time like you think they will. It took me years to get over it.'

'But this is different,' Kerr said. 'Georgie's chosen to leave. She's got a job lined up.'

'Not that different really. You have the chance to change things, but you have to be clear about what you want and let her know.'

Kerr let out a groan.

'Look, I'm not saying it's simple. Pursuing Georgie means more uncomfortable conversations with Jake are on the cards. But if you feel enough for her, then all the negative stuff will be worth it. And once you get over those barriers, you'll see that. Sometimes the brave choice is the messy one. The one that forces everyone – including Jake – to face truths they've been avoiding. Jake's lingering anger towards Georgie isn't healthy, and it isn't your responsibility to protect him from confronting it.'

'Ok, thanks.' He gave Eddie a hug, and Eddie patted his back.

'Believe me, you'll regret not trying more than anything else that might happen.'

He didn't want to live with regret. He didn't want to be walking up the street twenty years from now, explaining to some younger colleague how he'd once let the most significant connection of his life slip away because it was neater, cleaner, less complicated than fighting for it. He didn't want to wonder every time he heard Georgie commentating on tennis matches, what might have been if he'd found the courage to fight for her.

She might still choose London. She might still leave. But at least she would know exactly what she was leaving behind: a man who had finally found the courage to fight for what he wanted and take the risk, even if it meant incurring the wrath of his older brother.

Chapter Twenty-Seven

Georgie

Georgie packed like a soldier breaking camp. No hesitation, no sentiment. Clothes snapped into tight folds, shoved into the storage under the bed. Years on the circuit had stripped packing down to muscle memory – take what you need, ditch what you don't, move fast, don't look back. She didn't have time for nostalgia.

Her phone chimed with an email notification. Martin again, sending through the contract and schedule details with an enthusiasm that bordered on gloating. His earlier call had been all effusive praise and barely contained self-congratulation: 'I knew you'd make the sensible choice.'

Sensible?

Was any of this sensible?

She'd spent so many years having her life managed for her, and now she'd discovered it was necessary. Her first jaunt off alone and look what had happened?

What a mess.

A knock at the van's door startled her. She tensed, heart stuttering with the sudden, irrational hope that it might be Kerr. But he would be at work. Still, no one else had ever come here.

Georgie took a steadying breath before sliding the door open.

Elise stood on the gravel, in a tailored grey coat over slim black trousers.

'What are you doing here?'

Elise raised an eyebrow. 'I had a hunch you'd try to do a runner, so I thought I'd nip up and check you were still here.'

Georgie stepped back. 'Come in. It's cold out there.'

Elise climbed into the van, settling onto the bench seat and unwinding her scarf.

'Tea?' Georgie offered, desperate for the buffer of social ritual.

'No, thanks.' Elise looked around. 'This van is cute. Gabe has a roof tent, but this looks better. It has a kitchen and a bathroom for a start.'

'It is nice, but I've had enough now. A month in it has pushed me to the limits.'

'So you're leaving?' Elise raised an eyebrow.

Georgie nodded. 'Once I've packed, I need to go and see Amanda. She's asked me to call round to discuss something about the MUGA, but then I'm going.'

'Why?' Elise leaned forward, elbows resting on her knees.

'I've been offered a commentary opportunity. It's a really good springboard that could lead to bigger and better things.'

'I smell bullshit.' Elise's bluntness caught Georgie off guard. 'Something else is going on. You ran out on Saturday after you and Kerr went outside together. Then later, I saw Jake in the crowd. Why do I get the sense this has more to do with that than anything else?'

Georgie turned away, busying herself with folding a jumper that didn't need folding. 'Things have got too hot to handle.'

'So instead of facing that, you're running?' Elise tilted her head, waiting.

'I have to,' Georgie said. 'Don't you get it? If I was to hang about, it would just cause more and more hate between Kerr and Jake. My being here is like a grenade thrown into the middle of their relationship. No one will recover from the fallout. It could break their whole family. I can't be responsible for that, not when I'm already responsible for Jake being so upset and angry.'

'Ok, I get that.' Though her raised eyebrow said she was sceptical. 'But isn't there even a chance of working this out?'

'I wish there was. But I know what Jake's like. Kerr won't want to hurt him. Just like I didn't. I lived a lie trying to protect him, but it made it worse in the long run. I sacrificed what I wanted because I was afraid of upsetting him. But the way we broke up upset him more than anything else. That's why I wanted to come back and apologise. I can't begin to imagine how much pain I caused him.'

'But you're doing the same thing again.'

'He told me to go, so I am.'

'Kerr did?'

'No, Jake did. He'll cause so many problems if I go back. What if this pushes him over the edge? For all I know, he might be depressed enough to do something really crazy.'

Elise nodded. 'I work with his mum, and she's told me a bit about him.'

'Did she? And does she know about me and Kerr?'

'Yeah, she said on Monday that both Kerr and Jake had been with her on Sunday. They'd argued about you.'

'She must hate me.'

'No.' Elise ran her finger along her bottom lip. 'That's not the sense I got from her. She thinks Jake is in a really bad place because of his engagement breaking off. And she thinks this is him taking that out on the people around him. That's not to say he wouldn't have been annoyed by you and Kerr seeing each other, but it's all been made worse by this breakup. Apparently, this is what happened after the split with you. He dips really low, and it's tough for all the family – and everyone who knows him. People are afraid and walk on eggshells around him.'

'That's what Kerr said. But he always refuses to get help.'

'Kate wants him to get proper help and not have him take it out on the family this time, because it isn't fair on them – or anyone close to him – but he always refuses.'

Georgie fiddled with the cuff of her sleeve. 'So this could just go on and on?'

'Possibly,' Elise said. 'Though he might come around. Sometimes it takes a long time for people to realise something isn't right. God knows I spent most of my life making a mess of things – especially relationships.'

'I'm so clueless about them.' Georgie threw out her hands. 'What I had with Kerr felt so real, but how do I know for sure? What if it doesn't work out? Should I give up the chance of the commentary job for the unknown? I've never had to make decisions like this before.'

'Wouldn't everyone like to know that? I don't have the answers, but I read tons about love and what brings people together when I was struggling to figure things out. There's so much conflicting advice out there and so many opposing truths. Some people claim it's all about chemistry and you get an instant feeling about someone. Others say it's the opposite, and that chemistry is just lust and not something you can build a long-term relationship on. Some people believe in love at first sight, soul mates, cosmic connections. Others believe in taking time to let things grow organically, working hard to bring about the relationship you want – even if it's with someone you're not "chemically" attracted to. And within all that, there are different personalities, people whose core values are different, people whose sexuality is different, people who are at different stages in their lives. There's so much that comes into play. You could spend a long time over-analysing it. I know I did.'

'Until you got together with Gabe,' Georgie said.

A small smile softened Elise's features. 'Even after that. I'd spent so long disliking him that I was desperate to understand why my feelings had changed so much and if I was making a big mistake.'

'And do you think you are?'

'No. Because sometimes I believe you have to take a leap of faith. Not everyone would agree with me, but I feel like it's working for me. And one thing I know is that at least I gave myself a chance. If I hadn't been willing to try, then I'd have always had that niggle. The not knowing... the what might have been.'

The words lodged deep in Georgie's soul. She already had that sense. How often had she wondered what might have happened if she'd said no to Jake?

'What if it doesn't work out? What if I go back and the family breaks up because of me?'

Elise considered her for a moment. 'It's always going to be a possibility. But it could happen anyway. Kerr and Jake might be so annoyed with each other that they end up not speaking.'

Georgie threw her head back and rested it on the window. She felt suddenly exhausted, a heavy weight pressing down on her shoulders. Rubbing the injured one, she sensed the tension below the surface. 'I don't know what to do. I don't know how to stay and face all the complications.'

'Nobody does, not really.' Elise moved to sit beside her. 'We just have to wing it.'

Yep. No parents, coaches, managers, or agents to help her out this time.

'But I can tell you this. The people who matter are worth fighting for. Even when it's hard. Especially when it's hard.'

Georgie stared ahead. Options pinged up like balls waiting to be swiped away. Maybe she needed to pause before discarding them. Take a moment to make sure she gave herself every chance of happiness.

Elise had to go back to work, which was fine. Georgie needed some peace with her thoughts, especially when she had a meeting with Amanda later. Her insides did a funny flip. Would Kerr be there? But she knew the answer. He wouldn't be. Not when he was at work.

But why did Amanda want to see her then? It seemed silly for them to meet about the MUGA without Kerr or Finlay or anyone else who'd been involved.

The sharp trill of her phone cut through her thoughts. She glanced at the screen to see Amanda's name flashing. Hopefully she was calling to cancel. That would be really good because Georgie didn't feel like going to this meeting at all.

'Hi,' she answered.

'Georgie! Thank goodness I caught you!' Amanda's voice burst through the speaker. 'I have absolutely fantastic news, and I can't wait until later to tell you. I need to do it right now. Are you sitting down? You should be sitting down.'

Despite herself, Georgie smiled. Amanda's energy could be exhausting, but it was infectious. 'I'm sitting.' She perched on the edge of her bed. 'Is it the MUGA?'

'YES! ScotActive Trust has approved the project,' Amanda practically sang the words. 'Full funding, exactly as we proposed. They loved the community angle, and your support made all the difference. They said the application was perfect from start to finish and they didn't even have further questions.'

'That's wonderful,' Georgie said. 'But really, I didn't do much at all. You should take all the credit. You've worked so hard for this.'

'We all have,' Amanda said. 'And we're going to celebrate properly. I've already got a party planned for Saturday. Nothing too formal, just drinks and nibbles, and a chance for everyone who supported the project to pat themselves on the back. You'll be there, of course.'

The presumption was so typically Amanda that Georgie almost laughed. There was no question in her mind, no awareness that Georgie might have other plans – like, for instance, being back in London by Saturday.

'Amanda, I—'

'And I'd love if you could say a few words,' Amanda continued, steamrolling over Georgie's attempted objection. 'Nothing prepared, just a minute or two about what this club meant to you growing up, the importance of local facilities for developing talent, that sort of thing. The local paper will be there, so it's a perfect opportunity to get some positive coverage for the project before construction begins.'

Georgie ran a hand through her hair. 'Um... ok. I'll try.'

Amanda's delight burst through the phone like sunshine through clouds. 'Wonderful. I knew you wouldn't let us down.'

'Does this mean you don't need me to meet with you later?'

'Actually, that's about something else entirely. I would appreciate it if we could still meet. In fact, I'll nip out and get some things for the party. We can start setting up the clubhouse while we talk. Is that ok?'

Georgie wasn't exactly doing anything else. Not now that she was hanging around until Saturday. But that was it. She really couldn't do another minute after that.

Amanda was up a stepladder in the corner of the clubhouse, stringing fairy lights along the ceiling beams when Georgie arrived that afternoon – so much for it not being anything much. She'd already put up crepe paper streamers and a banner proclaiming the successful MUGA campaign.

'Ah, hello, Georgie. I thought I'd get started on this. I mean, it's Tuesday already, and that only gives me three more days. And I'm limited to the school day. Once the kids are home, I get nothing done. No one's really in much with the season being over, so I can leave it up.'

'You've done a great job so far.'

'Thank you. I called the other members of the committee at lunchtime to let them know. Kerr was very pleased, though he doesn't think he can make it to the party. Perhaps you can persuade him.' Amanda stepped off the ladder to assess her work. 'You and he seem to have developed a lovely friendship. And your mixed doubles partnership is the terror of the club. Together, you're unbeatable.'

'I don't think I'll be able to persuade him.'

'Pity.' Amanda moved towards a box of glass vases waiting to be filled with autumn flowers.

How much stuff had she managed to get in the space of a couple of hours?

'So... what is it you wanted to talk to me about?'

'Mmm,' Amanda hummed, arranging bronze chrysanthemums. 'Oh gosh, sorry. I've got completely carried away with all the party prep and the excitement about the MUGA.'

That much was evident.

'So what it is...' Amanda waved a flower stem like a conductor's baton. 'A wee birdie told me that you're a little uncertain about your future now that your tennis career is over. Which is quite understandable, I assure you.'

'Yeah...'

'The thing is, you've fitted in here perfectly. It's like you belong here. I know you grew up here, but your return has been seamless.'

'You think?' Georgie muttered. Clearly Amanda hadn't caught any of the Jake related gossip.

'Absolutely. The MUGA funding proves my point, but even without that, the fact you threw yourself so whole-heartedly into helping with it tells me how willing you are. And believe me, this community needs people like you. We've suffered too long with committees being run by... well, let's just say some shady people. The more fresh and enthusiastic faces we get, the better.' Amanda set down her flowers and fixed Georgie with a direct look.

Georgie gave her a little shrug, not sure if Amanda was going anywhere with this. Did she want her to join the club committee?

'The coaching you've done with my daughter and her friends is wonderful. There's a real demand for it. I think it would be great if you started doing coaching here. Obviously, you could charge privately. But I also think I could get more grants, so we could pay you to run camps and clubs. I have a lot of contacts at the local schools, so you could get involved with them too.'

For a moment, Georgie let herself imagine it.

A life here.

Coaching kids in the fresh air, running community camps in the school holidays, watching shy ten-year-olds grow in confidence with each swing of a racket. Early mornings at the courts, pub lunches with Elise, maybe even walking a dog she didn't own yet along the wooded paths behind the village.

But the image cracked as reality pressed in.

'Now that we've got the MUGA grant too, once that's built, you could do it all year round.' Amanda's voice still rang with enthusiasm, but Georgie's stomach tightened.

She'd already said yes to the commentary job. And that would be a much better paid option... But not even half as appealing.

Georgie cleared her throat. 'That's... really generous of you, Amanda. It means a lot that you'd even consider me.'

Amanda looked up, hopeful. 'So, is that a yes?'

'I need to think about it. A lot's happened. I'm probably going back to London.'

Amanda stilled. 'But why?'

'Some stuff happened between Kerr and me... and Kerr's brother.'

'What stuff?' Amanda frowned.

Georgie covered her mouth, and tears pricked. 'I've let so many people down.'

'Oh, now, now.' Amanda bustled over and put her arm around Georgie. 'You haven't. Something upsetting has happened; I can see that. But don't go thinking you've let people down. You certainly haven't let me down. Or the club. What you've done here is wonderful.'

'Everything just feels so messy. I don't know what I'm doing anymore.'

Amanda considered her for a moment, head tilted in assessment. 'I think that you've spent your entire adult life moving from place to place, tournament to tournament. I think staying put terrifies you. I thought you and Kerr had formed something special. And maybe you have, but does the thought of staying here scare you?'

Georgie hadn't really thought about it like that, but maybe Amanda had a point. 'I think the commentary job is an exciting opportunity, but it's also… an escape route.' It was a way to avoid dealing with Jake's anger and Kerr's divided loyalties and all the messy bits that came with staying.

'And what about your feelings?' Amanda asked.

A small, unexpected laugh escaped Georgie. 'I've kind of forgotten about them.'

Amanda pulled Georgie in for a hug. 'I understand. You've already become someone special in Glenbriar again, and that's probably overwhelming. The admiration you've had as a player isn't the same as really belonging in a place.'

She was so right. And not just belonging in a place, but with a person. The fun she'd had with Kerr. The way she could be herself with him was so alien and yet so nice. She didn't know where it fell on Elise's spectrum of love. To an extent, she'd secretly loved Kerr forever, but only in the last month, she'd come to see him as someone who she wanted in her future. Not for selfish reasons, but because he was someone whose company she enjoyed.

'I don't want to leave,' she said finally. 'But… my head is locked in a battle with my heart.'

'Don't be afraid of what your heart tells you. Sometimes it's better at decision making than your brain alone.'

Georgie laughed and pulled back from Amanda's embrace. 'Thank you.'

The path ahead wasn't clear, but hope had taken root in her chest – fragile yet persistent. If she wanted anything to happen, she was going to have to abide by her own rules. Feel the fear and do it anyway.

She couldn't do anything without first talking to Kerr, and that was proving difficult. He was busy at work, and she was helping Amanda sort out the party. The party that Kerr couldn't go to. What was he doing instead?

Georgie remembered where Jake and Kerr had lived as kids and toyed heavily with the idea of going around there and asking to see Jake, but that was an instant where she decided to listen to her head, not her heart.

She messaged Kerr again on Friday, telling him she was going to the MUGA party and after that needed to go back to London, but she really desperately needed to talk to him before then… if he would please let her know when.

All evening, she sat in the van, her heart aching, waiting for a reply that didn't come.

CHAPTER TWENTY-EIGHT

Kerr

Kerr marched up his parents' driveway. The familiar house with its neatly tended garden looked as pleasant as always, with the autumn colours shining through, but it felt like a battlefield.

That morning, he'd found a message from Georgie that she'd sent the night before. What a dick he must look not having replied to it, but he'd been so exhausted after school and with the lack of sleep that week that he'd hit the sofa and crashed. But he'd rectified that as soon as he woke up and replied to tell her he would try to make the party that afternoon. Then they could talk. But before he did that, he needed to speak to Jake. Maybe if his parents were there, it might be easier... or maybe he was just clutching at straws.

Opening the door, he peered around. 'Hello. Anyone home?'

'Kerr.' His mum peered around from the living room. 'We're all in here. Come through.'

With his stomach completely knotted, he headed through.

The living room was warm, almost uncomfortably so. Douglas sat in his customary laid-back way, but he was fooling no one. His gaze was fixed on Jake, who stood by the window, tapping his thigh.

'That goal should never have been allowed,' Douglas said. Typical Dad doing his best to jolly people along, but he may as well have been talking to himself. Jake didn't look like he'd heard or cared.

'Hey.' Kerr flung himself onto the sofa next to his dad. 'What goal are you talking about?'

'The Saints match the other night. Did you see it?'

'Na.' Kerr shook his head. 'The first week back is always exhausting. I've pretty much crashed every night this week.'

Jake folded his arms. 'Yeah? Like we don't know who you were crashing with.'

Douglas cleared his throat. 'Jake. Come on. Let's not start a fight.'

'I didn't.' Jake slumped into a chair. 'The fight was started for me.'

'Actually, that's why I'm here. To talk about this properly. I need to say a few things—'

'What is there left to say?' Jake threw out his hands. 'Georgie dumped me in a really callous way. Then, when she turned up here wanting to speak to me, and I explicitly said no, she turned her attention to you. And to cap it all, you went along with it. So now not only do I have to deal with the split from my fiancée, but also the fact that my brother and my ex are cosying up together.'

Kate perched on the arm of a chair. 'Darling, I think you've taken this out of proportion. While I don't agree with all Georgie's choices, Kerr has just been friendly to her, that's all? Isn't it? There's no question of anything else.'

Kerr rubbed his forehead. 'Actually—'

'Here we go.' Jake's voice rose slightly. 'I knew it.' Then he muttered, 'You always wanted to get your hands on her.'

Kerr's tether of patience snapped. 'Stop making this about you,' he said. 'Not everything is about you.'

Douglas eyeballed Jake. 'He's right. It's time you piped down and listened.'

'Thanks, Dad.' He turned to Jake, meeting the fire in his brother's eyes. 'You need to hear this. I didn't plan this. Neither did Georgie. But you're right about one thing, I did always "want to get my hands on her".' He made quotation marks in the air with his fingers. 'And you know it. You know that I liked her from way back – before you did. I think you only asked her out to get at me because you didn't get picked for the tennis team.'

'That's rubbish. You were just a kid.'

'So were you. You're only twenty months older than me, but because you were in the same school year as her and not considered a minor anymore, it was ok.'

Jake smiled, though it didn't reach his eyes. 'Clearly she didn't return your feelings. Otherwise, why would she have said yes to me? Why would she have stuck with me all those years?'

Kerr shook his head. 'I could tell you, but you won't like it.'

'Oh, do tell. Because no doubt she's made up some ridiculous story.'

'It's not ridiculous. She just didn't have the nerve to say no. She wanted to break up with you when she left Glenbriar, but you wouldn't let her go.'

'Let her?' Jake threw out his hands. 'I'm not her keeper.'

Kerr took a deep breath. He knew that was true. But he also knew what it was like to be afraid of Jake's moods. He'd spent years trying to appease his brother and keep him happy – they all had. It was easy to understand why Georgie had wanted to do the same.

'Look, all this happened when you were very young,' Kate said.

'Exactly,' Kerr said. 'And what's happening now is not about your past with her, or some twisted attempt to hurt you. It's about two people who connected.'

Jake's laugh was sharp. 'Connected? Is that code for saying you shag—'

'Jake.' Douglas eyed him. 'That's not nice.'

'Accurate though.'

'Maybe it is.' Kerr eyed Jake. 'But it's more than that. I didn't try to befriend her. The opposite. I pushed her away to start with, but circumstances brought us together, and I'm glad. Because we're good together. You don't know her anymore, Jake. You're holding onto a version of Georgie from years ago. And like Mum says, we were all really young. None of us did everything perfectly.'

'Do you have any idea what she did to me? How she left?'

'Obviously I do.' Kerr held his ground. 'Because you're obsessed with it. But you should have spoken to her about it when she tried. She wants to apologise. That was her whole reason for coming here in the first place. Why not let her say her piece? Or are you scared about what you might hear?'

'Why would I be?'

Kerr shrugged. 'No idea. But why else is it such a big deal? Why aren't you willing to hear her out?'

Jake narrowed his eyes.

'You need help, Jake. I'm just going to come out with it. I know you won't listen, but don't say we haven't tried. These moods, the anger, the negativity – it's all on you. Instead of blaming everyone else, get yourself sorted.' Kerr checked the time on the clock, ignoring Jake's red face. 'I need to go. I need to get to the club. I want to speak to Georgie before she goes back to London.'

'She's going back to London?' Kate said.

'Because Jake told her to leave his family alone, and she's scared.' Kerr's chest contracted like someone was crushing his heart. 'Another reason you need professional help.'

'Quit saying that,' Jake muttered.

'I'll stop saying it when you do it. I won't be quiet about this ever again.'

'He's got a point, Jake.' Douglas let out a sigh. 'You're a real mess, and nothing we do ever makes a difference.'

With a deep breath, Kerr got to his feet. 'I'm going. See you whenever.'

'Just let her go back to London and be free of her,' Jake muttered.

'No. I can't do that.'

'Why not?'

'Because I love her.'

Douglas and Kate turned around, staring at him.

'It's that serious?' Douglas asked.

Kerr nodded. 'Yeah. It is.'

'You love her?' Jake ran a hand through his hair.

'Yeah. I do. Now, I need to go.'

He said a quick goodbye and left.

The tennis club was only a short walk from Arden Crescent. Amanda was standing near the clubhouse, chatting excitedly to what looked like a reporter. Kerr's eyes, however, were drawn past her to the courts. Georgie was crouched down, talking to a group of children.

Kerr opened the gate and made his way onto the court. The kids all dispersed, and Georgie was packing balls into tubes.

She looked up at his approach.

'Kerr... You're here.'

'Yeah. How are you?'

'I've been better.' She popped another ball into the tube. 'We need to talk.'

'I know. Where should we go?'

She sucked on her lip. 'We could go for a walk around the back.'

'Ok.' He turned to walk back and his eyes fell on some people approaching from the path. 'Oh, no way.'

'What?' Georgie followed his sightline. 'Oh god. It's Jake'

Kerr nodded. 'And my parents. Seriously, this is not the right time. Let me go and tell them to leave.'

Georgie glanced towards the fence. 'Actually, no.'

'What do you mean, no?'

She took a steadying breath that raised and lowered her shoulders beneath her white dress. 'I'm going to speak to him and say what I wanted to say when I came here.'

'I'm not sure that's a good idea.'

'I need to do it.' She laid down the tube of balls and made to walk away.

'Wait.' Kerr took hold of her wrist, glancing around.

Georgie's eyes widened a little as she watched him. 'What?'

'I just want you to know… I love you.'

Georgie's lips parted in surprise, her breath visibly catching. 'Wow… Kerr.'

'I know it's too soon,' he said. 'I know you're not sticking around. But I can't let you leave without telling you how I feel.'

Her eyes shimmered in the pale afternoon light, emotions moving too quickly across her face for him to track. He reached for her hand, relieved when she didn't pull away.

'I wish we could find a way to make this work,' he said. 'I wish you would stay, or that I could follow you to London, or that we could find some impossible middle ground. Because the alternative – just letting this end before it's really begun – feels unthinkable.'

Georgie swallowed visibly, her free hand lifting as if to touch his face before hesitating in midair. 'Let me talk to Jake first. Once that's done, we'll see where we stand.'

She moved towards Jake, smoothing her dress with unsteady hands. Kerr watched her go, his insides tied in a knot.

Chapter Twenty-Nine

Georgie

I love you.

Kerr's words hung before Georgie like a second serve teetering on the net. Would it go over and give her another chance? Or would it fall back at her feet and lose her the point?

People in her life rarely used those words or expressed that sentiment. Love was what she got from fans when she was playing well. But that kind of love was an instant serotonin boost that quickly faded. What Kerr was offering was something more substantial and long lasting.

His parents were waiting by the fence, politely pretending not to watch her approach. But there was no way she could get to Jake without passing them. She turned to see Kerr still in the middle of the court looking lost.

Kate had a gentle smile, very like Kerr's. Douglas was rubbing the back of his neck.

Georgie slowed as she reached them. 'Hi.'

'Hi.' Kate gave her a little wave. 'It's nice to see you back. You've done good work with the MUGA application. We, um, thought we'd come along and...' She trailed off as Georgie's eyes fell on Jake.

'Thanks. But it was mostly because of Amanda. She did the majority of the work,' she replied, still looking at Jake.

'Could you give me a moment with Jake, please?'

Kate reached out, gave her forearm a gentle pat. 'Of course. We'll be just here.'

Georgie drew in a slow breath, her heart hammering against her ribs like a trapped bird. 'Hey,' she said.

Jake raised his chin by way of a greeting.

'I... um...'

'Awkward this, isn't it?' Jake gave her a self-deprecating grimace. 'But then, it always was a bit like this between us, wasn't it?'

'Yeah. It was.' Though it was the first time he'd admitted it. The wish that she'd had the strength to split up with him when she'd left Glenbriar rose to the forefront of her mind again. 'And that's kind of what I want to talk about.'

'Is it?' He kicked absently at the gravel beneath his feet. 'I thought you wanted to apologise.'

'I already did. At the Loch View Hotel. I said I was sorry, but you didn't want to hear it. I'm fine with saying it again though, because I really am sorry. I'm sorry about how I split up with you.'

'Uh-huh.'

'Yes. I really am. I should have told you myself and not left it to others. I get that hearing it on TV was horrible.' She looked up at him, meeting his eyes directly. 'But there are some other things I want to say if you'll hear me out. I'm not trying to defend my actions, but I'd like to explain them, if you'll listen.'

'Sure, whatever.' He sighed, running a hand through his hair.

'Well, you've acknowledged that things were always a bit awkward between us. And that was my fault too. With hindsight, I shouldn't have gone out with you in the first place.'

'Wow. How to hit a guy when he's down.'

'I don't mean to. And to be honest, we were so young, I didn't expect anything to come of it. When I left for London, I tried to break things off with you.'

'Yeah, I know.'

'But you pleaded with me and I... Well, I felt so bad about it. Even though in my heart I was ready for us to end. I should have ended it there, Jake. The situation with Stefan was so hurtful to you. I know it was. It wasn't even real. My manager set it all up for publicity.'

'I worked that much out.'

'I wondered if you would. I went along with it for the press coverage but also because I wanted out.'

Jake huffed.

'I never set out to hurt you.' And she hated that the way she'd handled it had caused him so much pain. 'But I didn't want to be with you either. I'm not right for you, and you're not right for me.'

'Apparently, I'm not right for anyone.'

'Then maybe you should try sorting yourself out before you go looking.'

'What is it with people saying that?'

'Well, if I'm not the only one, then maybe you should listen. If one person told me my serve was off, I might ignore it, but if two, three or more said it, then it would make me wonder. Maybe it's time you did the same.'

He gave her a look through slightly narrowed eyes, then turned away. 'Is that all?'

'Yeah.'

No words could make him feel any better, and she wasn't going to try. She knew others closer to him had it hadn't worked, and anything she said would be nothing more than a platitude.

She turned towards the clubhouse. Kerr wasn't on the court anymore.

'Where's Kerr?' Georgie asked his mum.

'He went inside with Eddie.'

'Thanks.'

Georgie pushed through the clubhouse door, the sudden wall of sound and warmth enveloping her. The room was crowded, a press of bodies and voices. She scanned the room, searching for Kerr among the celebration.

She edged past a cluster of tennis club committee members, murmuring apologies as she continued her search. People nodded and smiled as she passed, some reaching out to touch her arm or offer congratulations on her assistance in securing the MUGA funding. She acknowledged them, but her attention was elsewhere. Where was he? The room wasn't that large.

'Georgie! There you are.' Amanda's voice cut through the ambient noise like a precision serve. 'I've been looking everywhere for you.'

'Amanda, I just need to—'

'The raffle!' Amanda interrupted, linking her arm through Georgie's with gentle but inexorable force. 'We're about to announce the winners, and everyone's expecting our special guest to do the honours.'

How Amanda had even organised a raffle in such a short space of time was testament to what a bulldog she was. Once she got hold of an idea, she just wouldn't let go.

Georgie glanced longingly around the room. 'Can it wait just five minutes? I really need to speak to Kerr.'

Amanda's expression was sympathetic but unyielding. 'It won't take long. And Kerr isn't going anywhere. I saw him chatting with Eddie.'

The thought of delaying her conversation with Kerr for even a few more minutes made Georgie's stomach twist with impatience. After all the time wasted, all the uncertainty and missed chances, it seemed unbearable to wait any longer. But Amanda was already steering her towards the small platform at the front of the room.

'Fine,' she conceded, allowing herself to be led.

Amanda beamed, handing Georgie a list of prizes and a bowl of folded raffle tickets. 'Just announce each prize, draw a ticket, and read out the number. Couldn't be simpler.'

As Georgie stepped onto the platform, her gaze swept across the room one more time and there was Kerr near the back wall, deep in conversation with Eddie, his profile to her as he gestured expressively about whatever they were discussing. Even from this distance, she noted the tension in his shoulders, the slight furrow between his brows. He hadn't spotted her yet.

Amanda tapped the microphone, the feedback drawing the room's attention. 'Ladies and gentlemen, if I could have your attention once more. It's time for our raffle drawing, and we're delighted to have our very own Georgie Porter doing the honours. Many of you have been very generous with your ticket purchases, and we have some wonderful prizes to give away. Georgie, over to you.'

With a final encouraging smile, Amanda stepped back, leaving Georgie alone in front of the expectant crowd. She moved to the microphone, the list of prizes clutched in her fingers. The sight of all those faces turned towards her – familiar and unfamiliar, all part of the community she'd been welcomed back to – made her throat tighten. This wasn't a post-match interview or a sportswear promotional event. This was personal and felt even more important, especially if she wanted to put down more permanent roots here.

'Thank you, Amanda,' she said. 'Let's get started with our first prize – afternoon tea for two at the Loch View Hotel.'

She reached into the bowl, drew a ticket, and read out the number. A cheer went up from near the door as someone recognised their winning ticket. Georgie smiled, waiting for the winner to come forward and claim their voucher from Amanda. As she continued through the prizes – a hamper from Duchan Fayre, a whisky tasting experience at the Glenbriar Distillery, a riding lesson at the Glenvorneth Estate – her attention kept returning to Kerr, who had finally noticed her on the platform.

He'd moved slightly, turning to face her directly, their eyes meeting across the crowded room. The intensity of his gaze made her breath catch. He looked uncertain. Georgie smiled at him, and Eddie put his hand on Kerr's shoulder rather protectively.

She really couldn't wait another second to tell him.

'And now for our grand prize.' She recovered herself and read from Amanda's list. 'An eighteen-year-old Highland single malt, generously donated by Gavin Sinclair, the owner of the Glenbriar distillery.'

She drew the final ticket. 'Eddie Caldwell.' Her eyes widened as she saw the name scrawled on the back.

Eddie let out a cheer and came over. People patted his back, and he grinned widely as he thanked Amanda and shook her hand. When he glanced at Georgie, he winked, wielding the elegant box containing the bottle above his head like he'd just won a tournament.

Instead of stepping away from the microphone as Eddie returned to the crowd, Georgie remained where she was. Amanda, standing to the side, tilted her head in mild confusion.

'Before we end this party,' Georgie said, 'I'd like to say a few more words, if you'll indulge me.'

The room quieted, faces turning back towards her with curiosity. Kerr hadn't moved, his eyes still fixed on her.

'When I first returned to Glenbriar, I thought I was just passing through. Another stop on a journey that's taken me from tournament to tournament, city to city, never staying anywhere long enough to put down roots.' She paused, gathering herself. 'I've spent my whole life moving forward, always looking for the next opportunity, the next challenge, the next escape route when things got complicated.'

She glanced at Amanda and smiled.

'Thanks to a chance meeting at the hairdresser, I was lucky enough to meet Amanda, who reintroduced me to this club, and told me about the MUGA project. I was happy to get involved and I appreciate all the thanks people have given me today, but I hope everyone realises that the lion's share of work was done behind the scenes by Amanda, so please, let's give her the appreciation she deserves.'

Everyone clapped and cheered, while Amanda blushed and tried to step away as Georgie beckoned her over. Finally, she came up and took over the microphone, thanking everyone for coming and naming everyone who had taken part in the funding application process.

Georgie's eyes found Kerr's across the room, and suddenly it was as if they were the only two people present.

'And that's about it,' Amanda said.

'If I could just say one more thing.' Georgie reclaimed the microphone from her. 'The MUGA project represents investment in Glenbriar's future. And I've realised that's what I want too – a future here, in this community that's welcomed me back with such warmth and generosity.'

A murmur rippled through the crowd, faces showing surprised delight at her declaration. Amanda, at the edge of the platform, looked positively delighted.

'So I wanted you all to know that while I plan to do some part-time commentary, I'll be looking for a permanent residence in Glenbriar. Amanda suggested I get involved in local level coaching here, and that's something I've started doing with a few children here already, and I'd like to keep that going. But also...' Georgie continued, her eyes never leaving Kerr's. 'I want to stay because I've found something I value more than any job opportunity or career advancement.'

The murmurs in the crowd got louder, and people were looking around, clearly wondering what she was talking about. Kerr's expression transformed, disbelief giving way to a smile. Eddie was back at his side, and he clapped him on the back, still clinging to his whisky.

'If you want to build something lasting,' she said, voice trembling, 'you have to stop waiting for a perfect moment. You just have to start.'

The microphone couldn't capture the final words, which were meant for Kerr alone, as he stared at her.

'I love you too,' she said, just loud enough for him to hear, handing the microphone back to Amanda. 'And I'm staying. For good.'

For a heartbeat, Georgie and Kerr simply looked at each other, her still standing at the edge of the platform and him at the back, the entire room suspended in a collective held breath around them. Then Kerr moved – perhaps because Eddie had shoved him – his expression shifting from wonder to a huge grin. The wooden platform creaked as he stepped up beside her.

Georgie's heart hammered against her ribs, every sense heightened – the slight woody scent of his aftershave as he drew closer, the warmth radiating from his body, the intensity in his hazel eyes that made her feel simultaneously exposed and perfectly safe.

'You mean it?' he asked, his voice low enough that only she could hear. 'You love me, and you're staying?'

Georgie nodded, unable to speak past the tightness in her throat.

'Aw, this is wonderful,' Amanda said into the microphone. 'I don't think we've ever had a moment like that in this club. And when better than at our celebration? Now we have two special moments to celebrate. Let me thank you all again for coming here today, and I wish you all a safe journey home.'

The crowd began to move and disperse.

Georgie stayed where she was, safe in Kerr's arms. Something broke open in his expression. 'I don't even know what to say. Other than... Well, do you want to go out with me?'

She grinned. 'You bet I do.'

His hands framed her face, and he kissed her, not seeming to care if people were still watching. She certainly didn't.

'So,' Kerr murmured against her ear, his breath warm against her skin, 'what exactly does "staying for good" look like? Because I'm guessing you're not going to be staying in Ayu.'

Georgie laughed. 'Definitely not. I haven't figured out all the details yet. Just the important part – that I'm staying. The rest we can work out together.'

'Together.' He gently stroked her face. 'I like the sound of that.'

'So do I.'

She'd spent years chasing victory, pursuing the perfect shot, the flawless match, the ideal career trajectory. But standing here, with Kerr's hand in hers and the genuine goodwill of the people surrounding them, she understood something she'd missed all along: this was the real win. Not a trophy or a ranking or a commentary position in London.

This feeling of coming home. Of staying. Of finally, beautifully, belonging.

Chapter Thirty

Kerr

November

Kerr stamped his feet against the cold, his breath clouding in the frigid late-autumn air as he checked the station clock for the third time in as many minutes. The sleeper train was running several hours late. It should have been here first thing, but due to problems on the line, it was almost lunchtime, and it still wasn't here. Four days without Georgie had been torturous, a reminder of how quickly she'd become essential to his life, how the cottage felt so hollow without her – and these last few hours, worst of all.

Several weeks had passed since the night she'd appeared at his door, when everything had changed. Jake was still living at home with their parents. Kerr had seen an upswing in his moods, which was possibly because Mum and Dad were good at looking after him. Mum said they'd managed to persuade him to see someone to talk through his recent breakup. Kerr crossed his fingers, hoping that would help.

A northerly wind cut through Glenbriar station, finding every gap in his coat. November had arrived with brutal efficiency, stripping the trees bare and painting the mornings with frost. Kerr tucked his chin deeper into his scarf.

The train announced itself with a distant rumble that Kerr felt through the soles of his boots. He straightened, attention fixing on the bend in the tracks where the Edinburgh service would first appear.

The dark blue train slid into the station with a squeal of brakes, windows bright against the gathering dusk. Kerr scanned each carriage as it passed, searching for Georgie.

The doors hissed open, and she was there waiting. She headed towards him, her steps quickening as the distance closed. Kerr's chest expanded at the sight.

'Hi,' she said, slightly breathless. 'Bloody delays. We sat for hours at Carlisle.'

'Hi yourself.' He drank in the sight of her. 'But you're here now and the screen test went well.'

Georgie dropped her bag and stepped into him. She beamed at him, undid his coat buttons and slid her arms inside his coat to wrap around his waist, face tilting up for a kiss that was enthusiastic enough to raise Kerr's temperature by several degrees. Her lips were soft, her body wonderfully solid against his after days of absence.

'It went so well.' A smile split her face. 'The producer said I had "natural presence" and "authentic expertise".'

'That's brilliant.' Kerr squeezed her gently. 'Not that I'm surprised. You were always great on TV.'

She looked up at him, a teasing light in her eyes. 'Did you watch a lot of my post-match interviews?'

'One or two.' He winked.

Georgie laughed. 'And I had a good catch up with my family. They think I'm insane moving back here, and they're very worried about me dating another Halley boy. You'll have to visit and explain yourself to them.'

'Oh joy. I can't wait for that.' Kerr bent to retrieve her bag, but really he'd face much more than that for her.

They began walking towards the exit, shoulders brushing, hands finding each other automatically. The station's Victorian ironwork and glass architecture stretched above them.

'This station is so cute.' Georgie looked around. 'It's like something out of a time warp.'

Kerr nodded, happy just to have her back. No doubt he'd get used to this. She'd be away now and then when she was commentating, but living here the majority of the time, striking a balance that worked, a way to remain connected to the tennis world without sacrificing her new life in Glenbriar. Without sacrificing *them*.

'Can we go into that bookshop before we head home?' Georgie asked, nodding towards the Little Station Bookshop. The small shop was tucked into what used to be the ticket office before machines had taken over. 'It looks really cute, and I love a good romance story.'

Kerr chuckled. 'Yeah, sure. I've not been in there for years.'

On the door were two handwritten signs. One said: *Help Required – Apply Within* and another in green glitter gel pen said: *NEW! WISHING CHRISTMAS TREE inside! Cast Your Wishes Here!*

'You could do that job,' Kerr said.

'I'll give that a miss. It's a cute idea, but I like what we have planned.'

The Little Station Bookshop hit them with a wall of warmth as they entered, the scent of old paper and wood polish wrapping around them. Books crowded every available surface – stacked on tables, packed into shelves that sagged slightly under their weight, balanced in precarious towers on the floor. The narrow staircase leading to the tiny upper gallery was partially blocked by a display of local history volumes that leaned against the railing like tired travellers.

A rather scatty looking woman with her white hair pinned to her head with a wacky headband presided over the chaos from behind a counter piled high with books.

'Which one of you is here for the job?' She looked up hopefully and a pug scampered out from behind the counter and greeted them with a wagging tail.

'Do one!' a parrot squawked from behind the counter, and Georgie jumped.

'Um… neither of us. We're just here to browse.' Kerr smiled, and Georgie tried not to laugh but gave the dog a little scratch.

'Pity. I really need some help.'

'Sorry about that.' Kerr and Georgie avoided looking each other in the eye, knowing they would get a fit of the giggles if they did.

Kerr wandered towards the mystery section while Georgie browsed the romances. The narrow aisle barely accommodated his shoulders, forcing him to turn sideways to avoid disturbing the carefully arranged displays. From across the shop, he could hear the woman behind the counter either talking to the dog or herself.

Georgie came up to him with a few books. 'Let me get these, then we'll go.'

The woman at the till didn't seem to know how to work it, and she put her glasses on and off several times as she keyed in the amounts on the old till.

'If you want to make a wish, you can try out the wishing tree.'

'Um… Ok. Christmas wishes already.' Kerr winked at Georgie, and the two of them went over to a little Christmas tree where paper baubles had been left next to it with a packet of glitter pens.

The woman smiled as they both took a bauble, still looking at each other.

'Should we just do one together?' Georgie asked.

'Ok… I suspect we have the same wish.'

'For a real happy ever after?' She grinned.

'I love that.'

Georgie wrote the wish, hung it on the tree, and they thanked the woman.

As they left the bookshop, bags of books in hand, the two of them giggled.

'If I'd known getting a job around here was that easy, I wouldn't have worried.' Georgie shook her head. 'Do you think the parrot comes with the shop?'

'No idea.'

'Remind me again why we live in a country where our faces freeze off in November,' she muttered, clutching the paper bag of books to her chest.

'Character building.' Kerr nudged her arm as they left the station for the car park.

The walk to his place wasn't far, just across the main road and up the hill. Kerr carried her bags, despite her reminding him that she was used to doing it. By the time they reached the door, Georgie's nose was pink, and the bag handle had started to rip.

Inside, the warmth welcomed them like the bookshop had, only without the looming risk of a toppling tower of military biographies or being accosted by eccentric shop assistants. Kerr tossed his keys into the bowl on the sideboard, kicked off his boots and held out a hand for her coat.

'Thanks.' Georgie peeled it off and handed it over. 'Do you always run a rescue service for frozen women?'

'Only the ones who buy romance novels in bulk.'

She grinned and padded through to the lounge, curling up on the sofa like she'd always belonged there. Kerr followed, grabbing the blanket from the back and tossing it over her legs before dropping down beside her.

For a while, they didn't speak. The quiet between them was full but comfortable. Kerr shifted to lie back, arm draped along the back of the sofa. Georgie scooted closer, fitting herself in against his side, her cheek warm through his jumper.

'You smell nice,' she murmured.

'And you taste nice.' His voice had dropped lower, rougher. He caught her hand in his, brought it to his mouth, and kissed the inside of her wrist. A flicker of breath escaped her lips as he pulled her closer, their mouths meeting in a kiss that turned quickly from sweet to hungry.

Her fingers curled into the front of his jumper, then slipped beneath it, tugging it upwards with a quiet urgency. He helped her, lifting it over his head and tossing it aside without breaking the kiss. She laughed into his mouth as he fumbled with the hem of her jumper, caught it awkwardly on her elbow.

'You're a menace,' she whispered.

'Don't you love it?'

'You know I do.'

Clothes disappeared between kisses and half-laughed curses, landing in forgotten heaps on the floor. The sofa creaked beneath them as Georgie straddled him. Outside, the winter afternoon deepened.

They moved together with a breathless kind of need – not hurried, but intense. Kerr tangled his fingers in her hair, her name a rasp in his throat as she clung to him, legs wrapped tight, breaths short and hot against his neck.

After they'd both hit the dizzy heights, they lay tangled under the throw, limbs cooling, her head rising and falling against his chest.

It wasn't until a car passed outside and headlights sliced across the room that Kerr blinked at the window and muttered, 'Bugger.'

Georgie lifted her head. 'What?'

'I forgot to shut the curtains, and it's getting dark already.'

She laughed. 'Well, that's going to spice up the village WhatsApp.'

He groaned. 'Please tell me that's not a thing.'

'Honestly, I have no idea.' She kissed his chest and nestled back down. 'How about we go and play tennis?' she said.

'Are you kidding?' Kerr raised an eyebrow. 'Now? You've still got energy?'

'Loads. I've been on a train all night and half the day. I need to move.'

'And hot sex isn't enough for you.'

'I fully plan to do a lot more of that when we come back.'

'My god, I don't think I have the stamina to keep up with you.'

But he shifted, and she got up. Why not? It was always fun to play under the floodlights. And really, he would do anything she wanted. It had taken such a long time getting here – getting *her*.

Every moment was special, and he would never stop wanting to make her happy.

Georgie

'Let's go and hit some balls,' Georgie said.

'I think you just did that.'

She giggled. 'Wait until we get home.' She raised her eyebrows. 'I've got a treat for you.'

'Well, in that case, how can I refuse? Bribery works wonders.'

'Just forty-five minutes,' she said. 'Then we can come back, have a cosy shower... And I'll give you a present you'll never forget.'

'Such generosity.'

Twenty minutes later, they strolled into the tennis club, the chill biting through her leggings as she hugged her racket bag to her side. The car park was empty, the building silent apart from the echo of their footsteps. Kerr flipped the switches in the small control box, and the floodlights flared to life with a satisfying thunk.

Light exploded across the court, a clean, blinding rectangle carved from the thick November dark. Georgie squinted, blinking against the sudden brightness as her breath clouded white in the air.

'We must be mad,' Kerr said.

'I haven't played under floodlights in ages.' Her voice carried in the stillness, a little thrill racing up her spine as she looked around. These courts were where she'd started her tennis playing journey. Now she was beginning a new chapter. Perhaps one of the young people in her coaching classes would go on to play at Wimbledon too. And even if they didn't, she'd done her bit for the town. It felt like giving something back.

'Don't worry, I'll go easy.' Kerr winked. 'Wouldn't want to humiliate Glenbriar's resident tennis celebrity.'

Georgie grinned, pulse already lifting. She unzipped her bag and pulled out her racket. 'Bold words from a man who's won exactly two games against me since we started playing together.'

'What? That can't be right.'

'I assure you it is.'

They warmed up with easy rallies, just enough to loosen her muscles and shake off the train-ride stiffness. The cold nipped at her nose and fingers, but her limbs loosened with every swing. She watched the ball, let her rhythm return. Perhaps a lot of her worries about giving up tennis had subconsciously been about not having anyone to play against anymore. Now she had a partner... not just for a budding romance, but for this too.

Finding someone who was willing to do this with her was so precious.

'Ready to stop messing about?' she called after sending a forehand skimming across the net.

'Absolutely.' Kerr spun his racket to decide the server. 'Your call.'

'Rough,' she said, already focused, eyes locked on the spin.

It landed smooth. Kerr smirked and collected the balls. 'My serve. Prepare to be amazed.'

The match began properly. The familiar thwack of strings against the ball echoed across the court, punctuated by their occasional groans or laughter. Kerr held his first service game, but Georgie locked back in and answered with a flawless love game of her own.

'Still think you're revealing your true form?' she asked as they crossed paths at the net, her chest rising with exertion, skin warm beneath her fleece.

'Just getting warmed up.' Kerr twirled his racket, all smugness. 'Thought I'd let you enjoy a few good shots before I crush your spirit entirely.'

Georgie laughed. 'Your trash talk needs work, Halley. Almost as much as your backhand.'

'There's nothing wrong with my backhand.'

'Your technique's fine,' she allowed, stepping into her receiving position. 'But you announce it every time with that little shoulder hitch. Might as well send me a text message saying, "Backhand coming, please return with extreme force."'

Kerr narrowed his eyes. 'Right. Now it's personal.'

They pushed harder. The temperature barely registered now. She was focused, alert, everything narrowing to ball, racket, movement. But Kerr managed to steal a point with a vicious little drop shot. She cursed under her breath as she lunged too late.

'That,' she admitted, 'was actually impressive.'

'Don't sound so surprised.' He grinned, and for once, she let him have it. He'd earned it. And really, she was pleased. The competition was good – obviously not anywhere near the standard she was used to, but Kerr had played for a long time, and he often surprised her with some great shots.

The final game was a blur of speed and strategy. His serve kicked wide, dragging her off court. She scrambled, catching it just right with a cross-court forehand that sent him skidding. He lobbed – defensive but clever – and she almost groaned. The spin made it awkward, forced her to adjust mid-air, but she still got the smash away. It rocketed back, fast and true, but Kerr was already diving, body stretched, racket slicing a desperate backhand.

Georgie was already moving. She charged the net, heart hammering, and caught his return with a delicate angled volley that dropped soft and sweet just over the net. Unreachable.

'Game, set, and match,' she announced, sucking in a breath, and tossing her arms in the air like she'd just won a slam. 'But you made me work for it.'

They met at the net, both winded and grinning, rackets tucked beneath their arms. She couldn't stop smiling. He'd pushed her hard, and it felt good. Not just the win. The way they matched. The way they could compete and still have fun.

'You're incredible to watch when you're playing all out,' he told her.

'You're not so bad yourself.'

'Not quite enough to win, though.' He zipped up his racket bag, then wiped the sweat from his brow.

'Ah well.' She swung her bag over one shoulder, the satisfied ache in her limbs proof of how much she'd earned that win. 'Some things never change. Me beating you at tennis is apparently one of them.'

He pulled her into his arms. She let herself fall into him, smiling.

'You can win the game,' he murmured against her ear. 'I've already won the match.'

Georgie laughed, the sound bursting from her like champagne fizz. Kerr grabbed her waist and lifted her straight off the ground, spinning her with dizzy speed until her bag hit the court with a dull clatter and she shrieked with laughter.

'What are you doing, you madman?'

'Lifting my trophy.'

'Are you comparing me to a prize?' She joked. 'Something you can possess?'

'I am totally possessed by you.' He grinned.

When he finally set her down, she was still breathless, her hair wild, cheeks burning with cold and happiness. He kissed her, deep and certain, and she kissed him back, wrapping her arms around his neck and pressing close like she'd never let go.

And maybe she wouldn't.

Because this was it.

Not the win. Not even the kiss.

It was the sense of belonging. Of coming home. Of being loved for who she was inside and not her public façade.

For the first time in forever, Georgie knew exactly where she was meant to be. And she was staying there.

The End

More Books by Margaret Amatt

Scottish Island Escapes

1. A Winter Haven

2. A Spring Retreat

3. A Summer Sanctuary

4. An Autumn Hideaway

5. A Christmas Bluff

6. A Flight of Fancy

7. A Hidden Gem

8. A Striking Result

9. A Perfect Discovery

10. A Festive Surprise

The Glenbriar Series

1. Stolen Kisses at the Loch View Hotel

2. Just Friends at Thistle Lodge

3. Pitching up at Heather Glen

4. Two's Company at the Forest Light Show

5. Highland Fling on the Whisky Trail

6. Snowdown at the Old Schoolhouse

7. Starting Over at the Crafty Bee Barn

8. A Surprise Proposal in the Rose Garden

9. Cutting it Neat for the Wedding

10. A Classy Affair in the Country

11. Mix Up under the Mistletoe

12. A Fresh Start on the Bridle Path

13. Last First Kiss at the Village Church

14. Fight or Flirt on the Scenic Route

15. Love Match on the Road Home

16. Christmas Wishes at the Station Bookshop

17. Faking the Grade at Glenbriar High

18. Summer Nights at Hillview Farm

19. Love Song at the Music Festival

20. Holly Dates at the Christmas Cottage

Love on the Edge – Barra Series

1. The Castle in the Bay

2. The Lighthouse by the Sea

3. The Gateway on the Sands

Acknowledgments

Huge thanks go to my wonderful husband for always supporting my dreams (and for patiently enduring all the writing chat that never stops!). And to my son, whose curiosity and enthusiasm for storytelling always makes me smile – watching him create his own worlds is one of my greatest joys.

I'm also incredibly grateful to the editors who helped shape this book, and to the fellow authors and friends who continue to cheer me on behind the scenes – your support means the world.

But most of all, thank you to the readers. Whether you've just picked up one of my books or have been with me from the start, I appreciate you more than words can say. Your messages, reviews, and recommendations keep me going and remind me why I love doing this so much. I hope these stories bring you as much joy as I had writing them.

Big love.

Margaret XX

About the Author
Margaret Amatt

Margaret has told and written stories for as long as she can remember. During her formative years, she spent time on long walks inventing characters and stories to pass the time.

Writing books is Margaret's passion and when she's not doing that, she's often found eating chocolate, walking and taking photographs in the hills around Highland Perthshire. Those long walks still frequently bring inspiration!

It's Margaret's pleasure to bring you the ***Scottish Island Escapes*** series, ***The Glenbriar Series*** and the ***Love on the Edge – Barra*** series. Each series features interconnected stories for those who enjoy inhabiting Margaret's world but each and every book can be read as a standalone if you'd rather dip in and out.

You can find more information about Margaret on her website or by signing up for her newsletter

www.margaretamatt.com